To Dr. Gish & Lolly:

Best wishes &
christian salutations

John & Svetlana Doughty
Port Republic, VA
(Jackson's Last Valley battle)
1-5-2000 AD

JACKSON'S VALLEY CAMPAIGN

This portrait of Stonewall Jackson is based on a photograph taken in Winchester in early 1862, just before the start of the Valley Campaign.

GREAT CAMPAIGNS

JACKSON'S VALLEY CAMPAIGN

November 1861 - June 1862

David G. Martin

COMBINED BOOKS
Pennsylvania

PUBLISHER'S NOTE

Combined Books, Inc., is dedicated to publishing books of distinction in history and military history. We are proud of the quality of writing and the quantity of information found in our books. Our books are manufactured with style and durability and are printed on acid-free paper. We like to think of our books as soldiers: not infantry grunts, but well dressed and well equipped avant garde. Our logo reflects our commitment to the modern and yet historic art of bookmaking.

We would like to hear from our readers and invite you to write to us at our offices in Pennsylvania with your reactions, queries, comments, even complaints. All of your correspondence will be answered directly by a member of the Editorial Board or by the author.

We encourage all of our readers to purchase our books from their local booksellers, and we hope that you let us know of booksellers in your area that might be interested in carrying our books. If you are unable to find a book in your area, please write to us.

 For information, address:
COMBINED BOOKS, INC.
151 East 10th Avenue
Conshohocken, PA 19428

Library of Congress Cataloging-in-Publication Data
Martin, David G.
    Jackson's Valley campaign: November 1861-June 1862 / David G. Matin
        p. cm. — (Great Campaigns)
    Includes bibliographical references and index.
    ISBN 0-938289-40-3
    1. Shenandoah Valley Camapign, 1861. 2. Shenandoah Valley Campaign, 1862. 3. Jackson, Stonewall, 1824-1863. I. Title. II. Series.
E472.6.M37   1994
973.7'31—dc20   94-41578
          CIP
Combined Books Edition   3 4 5

First published in the USA in 1988 by Gallery Books. This revised and expanded edition is published by Combined Books, Inc., and distributed in North America by Stackpole Books, Inc., 5067 Ritter Road, Mechanicsburg, PA 17055 and internationally by Greenhill Books, Lionel Leventhal Limited, Park House, 1 Russell Gardens, London NW11 9NN.

Printed in the United States of America.

Maps by Paul Dangel

Contents

Maps

Sidebars

Preface to the Series

*J*ohnathan Swift termed war "that mad game the world so loves to play." He had a point. Universally condemned, it has nevertheless been almost as universally practiced. For good or ill, war has played a significant role in the shaping of history. Indeed, there is hardly any human institution which has not in some fashion been influenced and molded by war, even as it helped shape and mold war in turn. Yet the study of war has been as remarkably neglected as its practice has been commonplace. With a few outstanding exceptions, the history of wars and of military operations has until quite recently been largely the province of the inspired patriot or the regimental polemicist. Only in our times have serious, detailed, and objective accounts come to be considered the norm in the treatment of military history and related matters.

Yet there still remains a gap in the literature, for there are two types of military history. One type is written from a very serious, highly technical, professional perspective and presupposes that the reader is deeply familiar with background, technology, and general situation. The other is perhaps less dry, but merely lightly reviews the events with the intention of informing and entertaining the layperson. The qualitative gap between the two is vast. Moreover, there are professionals in both the military and in academia whose credentials are limited to particular moments in the long, sad history of war, and there are interested readers who have a more than passing understanding of the field; and then there is the concerned citizen, interested in understanding the phenomenon in an age of unusual violence and unprecedented armaments. It is to bridge the gap between the two types of military history, and to reach the professional and the serious amateur and the concerned citizen alike, that this series, the *Great Campaigns of Military History*, is designed.

The individual volumes of *The Great Campaigns of Military History* are each devoted to an intensive examination of a particularly significant military operation. The focus is not on individual battles, but on campaigns, on the relationship between movements and battles and how they fit within the overall framework of the war in question. By making use of a series of innovative techniques for the presentation of information, the *Great Campaigns of Military History* can satisfy the exacting demands of the professional and the serious amateur, while making it possible for the concerned citizen to understand the events and the conditions under which they developed. This is accomplished in a number of ways. Each volume contains a substantial, straight-forward narrative account of the campaign under study. This is supported by an extensive series of modular "side-bars." Some are devoted to particular specific technical matters, such as weaponry, logistics, organization, or tactics. These modules each contain detailed analyses of their topic, and make considerable use of "hard" data, with many charts and tables. Other modules deal with less technical matters, such as strategic analysis, anecdotes, personalities, uniforms, and politics. Each volume contains several detailed maps, supplemented by a number of clear, accurate sketch-maps, which assist the reader in understanding the course of events under consideration, and there is an extensive set of illustrations which have been selected to assist the reader still further. Finally, each volume contains materials designed to help the reader who is interested in learning more. But this "bibliography" includes not merely a short list of books and articles related to the campaign in question. It also contains information on study groups devoted to the subject, on films which deal with it, on recordings of period music, on simulation games and skirmish clubs which attempt to recreate the tactics, on museums where one can have a first-hand look at equipment, and on tours of the battlefields. The particular contents of each volume will, of course, be determined by the topic in question, but each will provide an unusually rich and varied treatment of the subject. Each volume in *The Great Campaigns of Military History* is thus not merely an account of a particular military operation, but it is a unique reference to the theory and practice of war in the period in question.

The Great Campaigns of Military History is a unique contribution to the study of war and of military history, which will remain of interest and use for many years.

Stonewall Jackson and the Valley Campaign

Stonewall Jackson was already well on the way to becoming a legend when he arrived in Winchester, the principal town of Virginia's Shenandoah Valley, on 5 November 1861 to assume command of Virginia's Valley District. Just seven months earlier he had hammered into shape a motley collection of campanies that were to become the 2nd, 4th, 5th, 27th, and 33rd Virginia Infantry regiments. At the First Battle of Bull Run, on 21 July, he and his brigade stabilized the wavering Confederate line on Henry House Hill and so provided the foundation for the Southern victory at the war's first battle. In the elation that followed, Jackson became known as "Stonewall" and his men the "Stonewall Brigade."

Stonewall's military exploits in the next two years were to be extraordinary as he showed the genius that ranks him among the greatest generals of the Civil War. His skill and reliability soon earned him the position of Robert E. Lee's right-hand man, and it is indeed difficult to imagine the Army of Northern Virginia in 1862–1863 without him. Jackson's masterful handling of his men at Harpers Ferry, his tenacious defense at First Bull Run, Antietam, and Fredericksburg, his march around Pope's army before Second Bull Run, and his bold flank attack against Hooker at Chancellorsville all added to the great fame and glory he would win in the war.

But it was Jackson's campaign in the Shenandoah Valley in 1862 that gained him his greatest renown. In the space of ten weeks (22 March-9 June 1862) he marched his men up and down the length of the Shenandoah Valley, fighting five battles (of which he won four) and defeating three different enemy armies. In addition, his movements tied down over 70,000 enemy troop—a force over four times larger than his own—whose aid was badly wanted by Union Maj. Gen. George B. McClellan for his attack on Richmond, the capital of the Confederacy.

Jackson's accomplishments in the Valley Campaign were so brilliant that they have been studied ever since at West Point and other military academies world wide. Their fame has been indeed justified, but the passage of years and the near sainthood attached to Jackson's name after his premature death from wounds received at Chancellorsville have combined to becloud the individual events of the campaign. Though the final outcome of the campaign was successful, as were most of its engagements, Jackson did not have a master plan for the campaign when it began, nor did he wage a perfect campaign. During the course of his operations he made masterful use of topography, interior lines, the marching and fighting ability of his men, and enemy disorganization, but he also at times made strategic and tactical mistakes that cost him dearly. Jackson fought the campaign stage by stage, taking advantage of each opportunity as it arose to meet his general objective, the sidetracking of Union troops from the Federal drive on Richmond. This was his true brilliance—the ability to analyze quickly and accurately the changing conditions of the campaign as it developed, and to respond decisively to them.

CHAPTER I

Jackson Takes Command

5 November 1861–12 March 1862

*J*ackson was a very logical choice to send to Winchester in the fall of 1861. He was a native of western Virginia, as were most of his men, and he had commanded in the Valley District for a short period earlier in the war. In addition, his fame as one of the heroes of Manassas was sure to buoy up Confederate spirits that were sagging because of Lee's failure at Cheat Mountain in September.

Jackson's assignment to command of the Valley District came as part of an overall restructuring of the Confederate forces designated to shore up the defenses of Virginia. On 22 October Richmond created the Department of Northern Virginia, consisting of all Virginia north of the Rappahannock River. The commander of this new district was Gen. Joseph E. Johnston. Gen. P.G.T. Beauregard, Johnston's co-victor at Manassas, had been sent to Tennessee, and Gen. Robert E. Lee had been sent to South Carolina after his defeat in western Virginia. Johnston's assignment was to guard the northern approaches to Richmond and threaten the northern capital as best he could. Jackson's task was to watch Johnston's western flank. His Valley District was defined as the area between the Blue Ridge and the Alleghenies, and between the Potomac River and the city of Staunton, altogether covering about 5000 square miles. Jackson was to have relative independence in his command, but he would rather not have been in this post. The job he really wanted was Lee's former command in western Virginia, which included Stonewall's home town of Clarksburg.

Jackson left the encampment of the principal Confederate army, Centreville, on 4 November 1861 with only two men to accompany him on the journey to Winchester. Col. J.T.L. Preston, Jackson's assistant adjutant general, had been one of the founders of the Virginia Military Institute (V.M.I.). He would not serve much longer with Jackson, and would return to V.M.I. in December. Jackson's second original staff member was young Alexander "Sandie" Pendleton, a first lieutenant who had been an old friend of Stonewall's. The three officers traveled by train from Centreville to Strasburg and then pushed on to Winchester, which they reached about midnight. Jackson took command in Winchester without any ceremony on the morning of the 5th.

Jackson immediately realized that his position at Winchester was far from the best. A Union force of 4000 was at Romney (only 30 miles west of Winchester) and additional strong Federal forces occupied western Maryland. To face these superior enemy forces, Jackson had only 1500 untried militia. He felt that the best source for much needed reinforcements was Brig. Gen. William W. Loring's army in western Virginia. Accordingly, on 5 November, the very day he took command in Winchester, Jackson sent Colonel Preston to Richmond to request reinforcements on the grounds that the Valley District was "defenseless." The Richmond government promised Preston that Loring's men might be made available; in the meanwhile, Stonewall would be sent the Stonewall Brigade and the Rockbridge Artillery. It seems that the men of the Stonewall Brigade had been chafing from inaction and a desire to return to their native valley. Their departure from Centreville satisfied their desires as well as Jackson's need for more troops.

These reinforcements raised Jackson's army to a strength of 4000 infantry and artillery. He also had 20 guns, 1000 militia in three brigades, and Col. Turner Ashby's cavalry regiment of 34 officers and 508 men. Jackson posted the Stonewall Brigade four miles north of Winchester, while Ashby's cavalry picketed an eight-mile line from Harpers Ferry west to Moorefield. The militia, which Jackson judged to be less reliable, were held back to garrison Winchester. Their main job appears to have been to

The brilliance of Thomas J. "Stonewall" Jackson's 1862 Valley Campaign is still studied by tacticians today.

keep the rowdier elements of the Stonewall Brigade away from Winchester's liquor and women. Stonewall also enacted measures so strict that his men could not even visit their families in Winchester without special passes.

On 20 November Jackson proposed to Richmond the plans for his first offensive campaign as district commander. His goal was to surprise and eliminate the Federal force at Romney, which

Brig. Gen. W. W. Loring did not get along at all well with Jackson and was transferred to the western theater of the war.

was a thorn in his side because of its key position as a base for potential operations against Winchester. Capture of Romney, Jackson argued, would cheer Southern spirits while also giving him a springboard for further operations against the enemy. Jackson's formulation of this plan was typical of his aggressiveness and his belief in the adage that sometimes the best defense is a good offense.

Jackson needed two key elements to carry out his campaign successfully—the cooperation of Loring's Army of the Northwest, and the advantages of a surprise attack that could be achieved only through quick action. The campaign began badly when neither of these requirements developed to Stonewall's satisfaction. Jackson had no authority over Loring's army and so could not order Loring's participation in the campaign. Directions to Loring had to come from Richmond, and when these were finally issued, Loring was given the option of aiding Jackson or not. Loring was slow making up his mind though he finally consented to cooperate with Jackson at the end of November. Even then, he agreed to commit only part of his command and these men were so slow arriving at Winchester that Jackson feared the object of his campaign would be lost. While the Confederates dawdled, the Federals strengthened Romney's garrison from 4000 to 7000 men.

The Dam No. 5 Expedition

The now impatient Jackson decided to keep his troops busy with another small project while he waited for Loring's reinforcements. Ever since Jackson had shut down the B&O Railroad at Harpers Ferry in May, the Yankees had been using the Chesapeake & Ohio Canal to transport coal from western Virginia to Washington, D.C. Jackson was well aware that the canal depended on several key dams to maintain its water level. His scheme was to destroy one of these dams, No. 5, north of Martinsburg, and put the canal out of operation.

Accordingly, Jackson mobilized the Stonewall Brigade and one militia brigade before dawn on 16 December and headed north. As was his custom, he told no one, not even his staff officers or brigade commanders, where they were going. This habit of Stonewall's certainly did help maintain secrecy about his movements, but in the long run it hurt as much as it helped, because it gave his subordinates no time to prepare their own plans or expectations. This, of course, was of no concern to Jackson, since he did not want free-thinking subordinates and insisted on blind obedience to his orders by everyone in his command, from generals down to privates. Anyone who disobeyed him was subject to arrest and court-martial, and Jackson instituted more court-martials than almost anyone else in the Confederate Army.

Jackson's column reached Dam No. 5 late on 17 December and began preparations to break it open early the next day. Because of the method of the dam's construction, it was decided that cannon fire would not be sufficient to do the job; the dam would have to be opened up by human labor. The task was made difficult by enemy fire coming from across the Potomac. Jackson finally drew off the Union opposition by feinting a crossing of the Potomac upstream from the dam. The job of knocking a hole in the dam was speeded up by a special ration

Jackson was frustrated in his effort to destroy Dam No. 5 on the Chesapeake and Ohio Canal in December 1862.

of whiskey to the workers, many of whom had to struggle for hours in clammy mud and water. (This was an unusual issue for Jackson, who was a complete teetotaler and would not tolerate drunkenness in any form.) With the aid of this special whiskey ration, the mission was accomplished, and Jackson headed his troops for home on the 18th.

On the march back to Winchester, Jackson got into one of the worst predicaments he met during the war. His aide Henry Kyd Douglas later described the scene as follows: "After riding along some distance, the general spied a tree hanging heavy with persimmons, a peculiar fruit of which he was very fond. Dismounting, he was in a short time seated aloft among the branches, in the midst of abundance. He ate in silence and when satisfied started to descend, but found that it was not so easy as the ascent had been. Attempting to swing himself from a limb to

Confederate field officers in camp. Jackson was extremely demanding of his subordinates. Any failure to carry out orders could result in a humiliating court-martial.

the main fork of the tree, he got so completely entangled that he could move neither up nor down and was compelled to call for help. He remained suspended in that attitude until his staff, convulsed with laughter, brought some rails from a fence nearby and made a pair of skids to slide him to the earth."

When Jackson returned to Winchester, he was greatly disturbed to learn that Romney's garrison had by then been reinforced to 10,000, and that all of Loring's command had still not arrived. If he were to strike at Romney, he had to strike soon, before all chance of success was lost; he was aware that once the Federals consolidated their hold on Romney and repaired the nearby rail lines they would soon move on Martinsburg and so force him out of Winchester. To make matters worse, many of Jackson's men were becoming disgruntled by their inactivity and were homesick after missing Christmas with their families.

Loring's men did not all arrive in Winchester until the week after Christmas. Though their march had been a leisurely one, for they had been well fed and entertained by Valley residents during their holiday march, Loring's troops arrived in a disorganized state and without much of their equipment. To make matters worse, Jackson did not care much for Loring and two of Loring's three brigade commanders. Col. William B. Taliaferro (commanding the 1st Georgia, 3rd Arkansas, and 23rd and 37th Virginia) was a politician who owed his rank chiefly to his family and political connections; Brig. Gen. S.R. Anderson led three Tennessee regiments (1st, 7th and 14th) that would have preferred to be home rather than in northwestern Virginia. Jackson felt most comfortable with Col. William Gilham (commanding 21st, 42nd and 48th Virginia and 1st Virginia Battalion), whom he knew well as a fellow instructor at V.M.I. before the war. Nevertheless, despite his misgivings about Loring and his subordinates, Jackson was anxious to get into action.

The Romney Expedition

The long delayed Romney expedition finally got underway early on 1 January 1862. Things did not go well from the start. Loring's command and some of the militia left camp late, throwing off Jackson's time schedule and clogging roads needed by other troops. Then the weather, which had been warm for three days, suddenly turned bitter cold. Most of the men, who had foolishly left their overcoats in the baggage train, were suffering. The supply wagons were caught up in the traffic jam north of Winchester, and the troops found warmth only by sleeping in huddled masses like sheep. Jackson himself received a surprise when he took a few gulps of what he thought was wine in order to keep warm. His beverage instead turned out to be whiskey. "Old Jack" soon complained of being too warm, undid his coat, and talked with his staff more freely than at any other time during the war.

As Jackson's small army reached Pughtown, some eight miles northwest of Winchester, his men were uncertain whether their goal was Bath (about 25 miles further north), Romney (almost 30 miles west), or some other point in Maryland or northwestern Virginia. Their goal became more clear on 3 January, when they were ordered to take the road towards Bath. Jackson's plan was to strike Bath's 1400–man garrison with a surprise attack late on the 3rd. His militia was to hit the town from the west, while Loring led an advance from the south. Jackson's plans began to go awry when his militia stopped advancing because of some trees felled across the road they were taking. Then, when Loring's skirmishers made contact with the enemy, the former called off his attack in spite of Jackson's direct orders to press on. It seems that Loring was annoyed at not being informed of the purpose of the expedition, and so was not eager to push his men when they were hungry-just one more episode of the bad blood between Jackson and Loring.

By now Jackson had lost all the elements of surprise, but he remained determined to defeat and destroy the garrison at Bath. Even this simple goal escaped him. On 4 January his militia column was checked and then partially routed, while Loring failed to press his own advance with any determination. At length Jackson, now totally annoyed at the whole situation, took direct charge at the front. But it was too late. Though he finally occupied Bath, he did so as the Union forces fled for safety to the north. Jackson attempted to catch them and then seize Hancock, Maryland, but he was stopped by a combination of several factors—inefficient pursuit, several ambushes set by the enemy's rear guard, and the coming of darkness.

Jackson and his men spent the next two days threatening the Potomac River line from Dam No. 5 to the mouth of the Big Cacapon River. Jackson's real goal was the Union supply base at Hancock, Maryland, but enemy resistance and intense cold weather prevented him from crossing the Potomac. On 5 January there was more than six inches of snow on the ground, and two days later the temperature went below zero in an unusually brutal cold wave.

The weather in fact turned so harsh that Jackson had to give up all hope of taking Romney. Instead, he was hard-pressed simply to get his men back to Winchester safely. Cold and disease felled many more men than enemy bullets, and his frozen, hungry horses were unable to pull the heavy wagons and cannon along the icy, snow-covered roads. Jackson's weary army limped back to Winchester, so frozen and exhausted that Jackson feared he might not be able to defend the town from attack. Major "Bull" Paxton of the 27th Virginia, who later

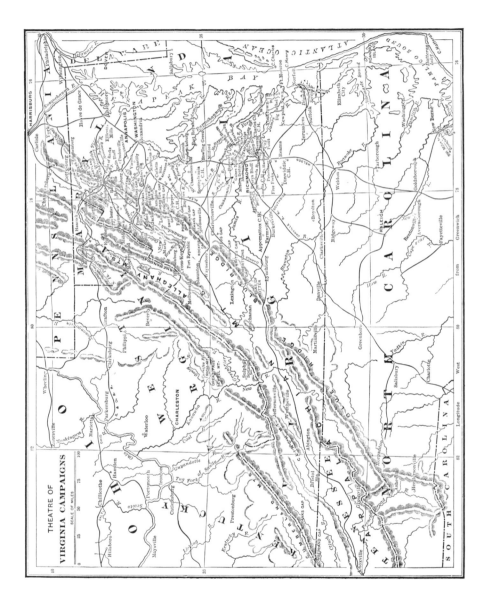

became one of Jackson's most aggressive colonels, hoped that Stonewall now had learned his lesson: "I take it for granted the general will come to the conclusion from this experiment that a winter campaign won't pay and will put us into winter quarters."

Then came a miracle. Turner Ashby, head of Jackson's cavalry, reported that the Federals had suddenly abandoned Romney, and that his own troops were holding the town. Apparently the Yankees had overestimated the size of Jackson's force, just as Stonewall had overestimated their strength. In addition, the bitter cold weather demoralized the Federals at Romney as much as it did Jackson's men. As a result, the Romney garrison was withdrawn to the Potomac line, which the Union command thought was much more defensible than the isolated forward outpost at Romney.

Jackson now needed only to march and garrison Romney if he wished to hold the town. The task was much easier said than done. It was sunny when he broke camp on the 15th, but by nightfall it was snowing. Over the next two days a severe sleet storm made it impossible for the men to march more than a few steps at a time. As a result, Jackson's troops straggled into Romney over a period of three days, from the 15th to the 17th.

Jackson was not content with the occupation of Romney. Before he arrived there he began forming plans to move against New Creek or Cumberland. When his exhausted men heard of his plans, they nearly revolted. Their regiments were already reduced to skeletons, and there was no way they could begin another offensive campaign. Reluctantly, Jackson recognized that his men were not made of iron, and he scrapped his plan; it would not be the only time that Stonewall's plans would be more ambitious than the ability of his men to carry them out. Jackson then dispersed his brigades to winter quarters. Loring's command was stationed at Romney with a militia brigade, while other militia brigades were assigned to Bath and Moorefield. Brig. Gen. Richard B. Garnett's Stonewall Brigade, by far the most reliable unit in Jackson's small army, was posted in strategic reserve at Winchester.

As events developed, the Confederates were to hold Romney for only about a week. Loring, whose brigade had been assigned to hold the town, had little liking for the hard driving Jackson and even less liking for the "disagreeable and unfavorable" town of Romney. He and many of his officers and men petitioned the Confederate War Office in Richmond to have the brigade recalled. They even went so far as to concoct stories about Federal movements that were threatening to cut off the place. These stories alarmed Secretary of War Judah P. Benjamin, who in turn persuaded President Jefferson Davis of Loring's predicament. As a result, on the 29th Davis directed Jackson to order Loring to abandon Romney.

Jackson was understandably irate that the Richmond bureaucrats so readily ordered him to abandon the town he had gained by such great effort. On 31 January 1862 he wrote the Secretary of War:

> Sir: Your order requiring me to direct General Loring to return with his command to Winchester immediately has been received and promptly complied with.
>
> With such interference in my command I cannot expect to be of much service in the field, and accordingly respectfully request to be ordered to report for duty to the superintendent of the Virginia Military Institute in Lexington, as has been done in the case of other professors. Should this application not be granted, I respectfully request that the President will accept my resignation from the Army.

Fortunately for the Confederacy, Jackson was at length dissuaded from resigning by John Letcher (the governor of Virginia), Gen. J.E. Johnston (his department commander), and numerous friends, including Congressman Alexander Boteler. The angry Jackson then turned his energies to preparing court-martial charges against Loring. His efforts were stymied when Loring was transferred to the Army of Mississippi, and by late February the whole affair had blown over.

Thus Jackson's first offensive campaign in the Valley ended with mixed success. He had succeeded in driving the enemy from Bath and Romney, so relieving most of the pressure on Winchester. But, because of Loring's machinations, he had been unable to hold Romney. His difficulty with Loring showed a trait that would continue throughout the war—Jackson demanded blind obedience from his lieutenants and did not share his plans with them. More subtle treatment of Loring might have avoided the entire Romney debacle. In addition, Jackson's winter campaign served more to break the back and spirit of his Valley army than to increase its morale and efficiency. At the end of the Romney campaign Loring's troops were so dispirited that his command was broken up—his Virginia units went to Joe Johnston's army, and his Tennessee units were sent home. Even Jackson's own troops were exhausted by the campaign, so much so that all they could think of was furloughs or resigning when their one-year term of enlistment was up in the spring of 1862. At the end of February Jackson could muster only 5400 men from a paper strength of 13,759; he had almost as many men sick or on furlough as he had ready for the battle line.

Foundation for the Great Campaign

Following the Loring affair, Jackson's position in the Valley went from bad to worse. The Federals had been more than pleased to see the Confederates abandon Romney, and they reoccupied the town without opposition on 7 February. Within a week the bridge over the Cacapon River was repaired and the railroad line from Cumberland to Hancock was back in operation. The Federals also occupied the key approaches to Bath and Romney, making it impossible for Jackson to threaten these points with the reduced forces at his command. During the month of February the Confederate Congress had authorized 30–day furloughs to all the one-year troops who reinlisted, and Jackson saw most of his best men go home for a month.

Jackson's position at Winchester became much more tenuous at the end of the month. In mid-February Union Maj. Gen. Nathaniel Banks' corps, which had spent the winter at Frederick, Maryland, was directed to move south and secure the lower Valley as a prelude to Maj. Gen. George B. McClellan leading his *Army of the Potomac* "on to Richmond" from Washington. Banks' advance forces occupied Harpers Ferry on 24 February. Over the next few days the rest of Banks' command crossed the Potomac, and Union outposts were sent out to Charlestown, Martinsburg, and Bunker Hill.

In response to this pressure, Jackson began preparations to fortify Winchester and increase communications with the Confederate garrison at Leesburg on his far right flank. He also wrote to Joe Johnston for help, but Johnston was in no position to offer any. He had major problems of his own. McClellan's greatly superior army was beginning to stir at Washington, and Johnston knew that he would soon have no choice but to abandon the Centreville and Manassas camps he had held all winter. He began moving his supplies out on 22 February and started evacuating his troops on 7 March. By 11 March Johnston's army was repositioned along the Rappahannock River west of Fredericksburg.

Before Johnston left Centreville, he gave orders for Jackson to fall back before Banks while continuing to guard Johnston's far left flank. Jackson, however, was not to lose contact with Banks for fear that Banks would leave a holding force, join McClellan, and help overwhelm Johnston.

Jackson had little choice but to follow Johnston's orders. Against Banks' command of over 25,000 men, Jackson had only 4000 infantry, 600 cavalry, and 27 cannon. Once the Confederate forces evacuated Leesburg and Manassas, Jackson's position was isolated and totally untenable. Banks' main force reached Bunker Hill, 12 miles north of Winchester, on 6 March, and on the 11th Col. John Sedgwick's Union division reached Berryville, 10 miles east of Winchester. With the nearest Confederate forces some 60 miles away near Fredericksburg, Jackson would be totally on his own. Joe Johnston's army was some 90 miles to the southeast, and Jackson's superior was not in any mood to lend him troops at the moment.

Jackson was well aware of his predicament, and began evacuating his supplies soon after Banks reached Bunker Hill. In order to mask his weakness, he formed a battle line north of Winchester on the 11th. He boldly dared Banks to attack, but Banks cautiously declined, even though he outnumbered the Confederates more than six to one. With the Yankees now held at a safe distance, Jackson very reluctantly abandoned Winchester late on the 11th. As his troops marched south out of town, Stonewall held a meeting of all his senior commanders. There he astounded them by announcing that he planned to turn and make a bold attack on the enemy the next day! He anticipated that the enemy would be disorganized and elated, and so could

Brig. Gen. Bernard E. Bee gave Jackson his nickname "Stonewall" at the battle of First Bull Run in July 1861. Some believe he meant it as a criticism rather than a compliment, but we will never know because Bee was killed before the battle was over.

easily be routed. Jackson's lieutenants, though, had no interest in such a maneuver. They pointed out that the army was then more than six hours south of Winchester, and would need to march all night in order to return for a daylight attack. Jackson was sure that his troops could carry out the attack, but his officers persuaded him otherwise. So, Jackson joined the army's retreat. But before he left the environs of Winchester, he paused to look back at the city and declare to his companion, Dr. Hunter McGuire, "That is the last council of war I will ever hold." And indeed it was.

The Valley in the Civil War

In 1862 the people of the Valley were staunchly Confederate in allegiance, though not many owned slaves. They were primarily a mix of old English settlers from the Tidewater and Scotch-Irish Protestants of the Piedmont-from whom Stonewall Jackson was descended—plus many thrifty Germans.

The Valley district achieved national prominence even before the war started. It was at Harpers Ferry that abolitionist John Brown made his last raid on 16 October 1859. Brown attempted to seize the United States arsenal there in order to arm slaves for insurrection, but he was himself captured—at the arsenals firehouse by a detachment of Marines led by Col. Robert E. Lee. Brown was convicted of murder and other heinous crimes, and hanged at Charleston on 2 December 1859, before a crowd that included 2000 Valley militia and the cadets from V.M.I.

As the war approached, the eyes of both sides were focused on the huge U.S. armory and arsenal at Harpers Ferry. Here were stored 17,000 finished muskets and all the tools and equipment necessary to make more. On 17 April 1861 Virginia seceded from the Union. Federal officials were well aware that they could not defend the arsenal from the hordes of militia that would soon swarm down on it. Accordingly, the arsenal and its buildings and guns were burned on 18 April 1861. The fire, however, did not consume all the machinery or metal gun parts. These the Southerners salvaged and transported to a newly established gun factory at Fayetteville, North Carolina.

The Confederates then occupied Harpers Ferry with a force commanded by Brig. Gen. Joe Johnston. Facing Johnston was a growing Union army under Maj. Gen. Robert Patterson. It did not take long for Johnston to realize that he would be unable to hold Harpers Ferry, so he withdrew on 15 June 1861 to Winchester. Patterson followed him, and by 15 July the Union army was at Charleston. There the Yankees were faced by J.E.B. Stuart's Virginia cavalry and by confusing orders from Washington. Johnston took advantage of the situation to slip away from Winchester and join Beauregard's Confederate army at Manassas in time to help defeat McDowell's Union army at the battle of First Bull Run on 21 July 1861.

The Valley was then held by local militia until Jackson was assigned to command in early November. Following Jackson's appointment, the Valley achieved importance for more than just its agricultural and industrial products. Primary Union strategy for the war was to attack Richmond. Any Confederate forces perched in the Valley would be able to swoop down on the flank or rear of an invading Federal army. Worse yet, the Confederates would be able to use the Valley as a corridor to invade the North, as they did in the Antietam and Gettysburg Campaigns, or even threaten Washington, as Jubal Early did in July 1864.

The geographic reality virtually dictated that the Valley would be an important battleground. And so it was. By one estimate, Winchester changed hands more than 70 times during the war. After Jackson's spring 1862 campaign, the Yankees kept control of the lower Valley. On 15 September 1862, during the Antietam Campaign, Jackson captured the Harpers Ferry garrison—commanded by Col. Dixon S. Mile—a prize containing 12,000 Yankees, 13,000 small arms, and 73 cannons. Another major battle occurred at Second Winchester on 14 June 1863, when Dick Ewell defeated Maj. Gen. Robert Milroy in the opening stages of the Gettysburg Campaign.

In 1864 the Valley once again became a major battleground. On 15 May Maj. Gen. Franz Sigel's invading Union army was defeated at New Market by a makeshift command led by Maj. Gen. John C. Breckinridge. A month later Breckinridge and part of Jubal Early's II Corps defeated Maj. Gen. David Hunter's invading army at Lynchburg. From there Early began a foray that led to victory at Monocacy, Maryland (9 July 1864), and his famous attack on Washington, D.C., at Fort Stevens (12 July 1864). Union troops then pursued Early back to the Valley and captured Winchester on 20 July. Early, however, recaptured the town after a victory at Kernstown on 224 July. He then raided Maryland and sent cavalry to burn Chambersburg, Pennsylvania (30 July 1864).

By then Grant decided that the Valley needed to be cleared of Confederate forces once and for all. On 7 August 1864 he sent Maj. Gen. Philip Sheridan to take command of the *Middle Military Division*, consisting of the *VI Corps, XIX Corps,* troops from West Virginia, and two cavalry divisions from the *Army of the Potomac.* Sheridan was faced by four infantry divisions in Early's reinforced II Corps. During this campaign the Confederates were so badly outnumbered that they never really had a chance.

The two armies sparred and maneuvered for five weeks before the heavy fighting began. Early was defeated at The Third Battle of Winchester (also known as Opequon) on 19 September 1864 and again at Fishers Hill, near Strasburg, on 22 September. He retreated in haste to Mount Jackson, but Sheridan withdrew down the Valley, destroying all the military facilities he passed. While Sheridan was virtually demobilizing, Early, in a bold move, attacked at Cedar Creek on 19 October, carrying the day until Sheridan made a mad dash from Winchester to join his men, arriving in the nick of time to change the tide of battle.

Cedar Creek was the last major battle in the Valley. Early now had only a skeleton force remaining, so most of Sheridan's troops were sent to other armies. The Valley's final campaign began on 27 February 1865 when Sheridan left Winchester with two excellent cavairy divisions. He drove Early south and then out of the Valley, occupying Staunton on 3 March. Sheridan then returned to Harrisonburg. From there he sent his cavalry to ravage the Valley and carry off or destroy all the food and militarily useful goods. He then withdrew down the Valley continuing his devastation, which rivaled Sherman's in Georgia, though Sheridan did not burn civilian homes. Sheridan's report to Grant notes the riches the Valley held, "I have destroyed over 2000 barns filled with wheat, hay and farming implements; over 70 mills filled with flour and wheat; have driven in front of the army over four herd of stock, and have killed or issued to the troops not less than 3000 sheep." These supplies were in addition to the following that were seized or destroyed in the fall 1864 campaign: 3772 horses, 545 mules, 10, 918 beef cattle, 12,000 sheep, 15,000 swine, 250 calves, 435, 802 bushels of wheat, 77, 176 bushels of corn, 20, 397 tons of hay, 20,000 bushels of oats, 10,000 pounds of tobacco, 12,000 pounds of bacon, 2500 bushels of potatoes, 1665 pounds of cotton yarn, 874 barrels of flour, 500 tons of fodder, 450 tons of straw, 71 flour mills, 1 woolen mill, 8 sawmills, 1 powder mill, 3 saltpeter works, 1200 barns, 7 furnaces, 4 tanneries, 1 railroad depot, and 947 miles of rail.

When he was done robbing and burning the granary of the Confederacy, Sheridan remarked, "A crow would have to carry its own rations if it had flown across the Valley."

Jackson's Ancestry and Early Life

Thomas Jonathan Jackson was born on 21 January 1824 in Clarksburg in western Virginia. His lineage was Scotch-Irish, the predominant stock of the early settlers of the Shenandoah Valley region. In 1748 the 23 year-old John Jackson, Stonewall's great-grandfather, had left London for America. Aboard ship he met and fell in love with an attractive - six-foot-tall blonde named Elizabeth Cummins. Elizabeth was indentured to a family from Calvert County, Maryland, whom she had promised to work for in exchange for the cost of her boat ticket. John Jackson settled in Baltimore and waited patiently for her term of service to pass. The couple were married about two years after their arrival, and moved to western Virginia to get a start on life. They settled first at Moorfields in Hardy County, later going farther west to a village on the Buckhannon River called Jackson's Fort, now Buckhan-

non. The area was wild and populated by hostile Indians, but the Jacksons stayed and prospered.

John Jackson and several of his sons served in the American army during the Revolution. In their later years, John and Elizabeth lived in Clarksburg, Virginia (now West Virginia). There John died at 86. Elizabeth, who was physically and intellectually the backbone of the clan, passed away in 1825, at the extraordinary age of 105.

John and Elizabeth began a closeknit family that achieved a fair level of distinction in western Virginia. John's eldest and most notable son was Col. George Jackson of Clarksburg. George won his rank as colonel during the Revolution, and later served in the Virginia legislature and U.S. Congress. While in Washington, he had the opportunity to meet Senator Andrew Jackson of Tennessee, the future President, and the two discovered that their families had come from the same parish near Londonderry, so that they were probably distant cousins.

George Jackson's son, John G. Jackson, was also a man of note, being a congressman and federal judge. His first wife was Polly Payne, sister of Dolley Madison, the wife of President James Madison; after Polly's death in 1807, John G. married the only daughter of Governor Meiggs of Ohio. John G. Jackson died in 1825 at the comparatively young age of 48. One of John G.'s sons, George Washington Jackson, was the father of Col. Alfred H. Jackson, who was mortally wounded at Cedar Mountain while serving on Stonewall's staff.

Stonewall was descended from John Jackson's second son, Edward. Edward's line was less distinguished than that of his older brother George. This was perhaps because of the great size of Edward's family. Edward, who was a surveyor in Lewis County, had no fewer than 15 children, 6 by a first marriage and 9 by a second. One of this brood was Jonathan, the father of Stonewall. Jonathan studied law under his more prosperous cousin, Judge John G. Jackson, and then became a lawyer in Clarksburg.

In Clarksburg, Jonathan Jackson married Julia Beckwith Neale, daughter of a merchant from Parkersburg. Her family had also been early settlers of western Virginia. One source describes her before Stonewall's birth as "rather a brunette, with dark-brown hair, dark gray eyes, handsome face, and when at maturity, of medium height and symmetrical form." Her husband, Stonewall's father Jonathan,

was "a man of short stature, with an open, pleasing face, blue eyes, and handsome mouth."

Jonathan and Julia Jackson had four children in their cottage at Clarksburg. Jonathan did well as a lawyer, but did not handle his income wisely. When he died in 1826, from a fever that also took his eldest child Elizabeth, his family was left in poverty. Young Thomas Jonathan was only 3 at the time, so he had no recollection of his father or the poverty his widowed mother lived in. For several years the small family lived in a one-room house loaned by the Freemasons, a society to which Jonathan had belonged. In the summers Julia took her three children to her father's home in the mountains in order to escape the heat.

In 1830, three years after Jonathan died, Julia remarried. Her second husband, Captain Blake B. Woodson of Cumberland County, was a lawyer of good social standing, but he was an elderly widower without much money. In fact, Julia's Jackson kin advised her against the marriage on the grounds that Woodson would not have the means to support Julia's three children. That is exactly what happened. Julia kept her youngest child, Laura, with her, but had to send her two sons to live with her relations. Warren was sent to live with an aunt, Mrs. Isaac Brake, and Thomas Jonathan with an uncle.

Julia died a year later. After giving birth to a son, Wirt, she weakened and passed away in the fall of 1831 at age 33. The whole situation—separation from his mother at age 6 and then her death when he was 7—made a lifelong impression on young Thomas Jonathan; he always spoke of his mother with tenderness, and named his only child, Julia, after her. In 1855 Stonewall sought her grave in Ansted, Fayette County, for the purpose of marking it. He wrote an aunt, Mrs. Neale of Parkersburg, describing the visit: "I stopped to see the Hawk's Nest, and the gentleman with whom I was put up was at my mother's burial, and accompanied me to the cemetery for the purpose of pointing out her grave to me; but I am not certain that he found it. There was no stone to mark the spot. Another gentleman, who had the kindness to go with us, stated that a wooden head or foot board with her name on it had been put up, but it was no longer there. A depression in the earth only marked her resting place. When standing by her grave, I experienced feelings to which I was until then a stranger." Jackson did not mark his mother's grave then because he was uncertain of its exact location and because he had no money after losing his wallet. Nor did he have the opportunity to return later. The grave of Julia Neale Jackson Woodson was finally marked after the war by one of Stonewall's former soldiers, Captain Thomas D. Ransom of Staunton.

After their mother died, Laura and Thomas lived for awhile with an aunt, Mrs. White, and then with their step-grandmother, Mrs. Jackson. She treated them kindly until she died. Laura was sent to live with her Neale relations. She later married Jonathan Arnold of Beverly, Virginia and had two sons, Thomas Jackson Arnold and Stark W. Arnold, Stonewall's only nephews.

Following the death of his Grandmother Jackson, Thomas J. stayed at her house, which passed to his uncle, Cummins Jackson. Cummins was a large, big-hearted man, and was about the only relative to show any great interest in Thomas' upbringing. Cummins also took an interest in Thomas' brother Warren, after Warren at age 9 or 10 ran away from the Brake family, who had taken him in. Cummins treated the boys as his own sons, and particularly favored Thomas. Thomas thrived, working hard at school and at the violin, one of the few things he attempted but could not master. Warren, however, proved to be restless, and left his foster home in 1836 at age 14. The sad thing was that he persuaded Thomas, age 12, to come with him. The two spent the summer kicking around Ohio, spending some of their time with relatives and the rest on their own. Finally things got so bad that they returned east, aided by a kind boat captain who gave them passage. Thomas was accepted by Uncle Cummins as a prodigal son. Warren, though, was too proud and went to live with the Brakes again. There he began withering from ill health, and died of consumption at age 19.

Thomas thrived under his uncle's tutelage, attending school when he could and helping to administer the farm. It was a happy time for him, but he was all too aware that he had little means or formal education to earn a good career. At age 18 his uncle won him appointment as constable of Lewis County. Thomas did not enjoy the job, which included collecting debts. Consequently he sought and earned an appointment to West

Point in order to better himself. In 1842 he left Uncle Cummins to live on his own. Uncle Cummins a few years later was caught up in the fever of the California gold rush and went west by wagon train, even though he was 50 years old. He survived in California only a few months. Thus Thomas lost his foster father and best supporter soon after he applied to West Point.

Jackson's First Command in the Valley

Jackson's first command in the Shenandoah Valley began on 30 April 1861. He had recently been commissioned a colonel of Virginia troops, and was sent by the state's governor, John Letcher, to take charge of the forces at Harpers Ferry. There Jackson found a tangle of militia, 12-months volunteers, and volunteers enlisted for the "duration." The whole mob badly needed organizing and drilling. They also needed weapons, which Jackson finally had to requisition from arsenals in Lexington, Virginia.

Jackson's first "campaign" foreshadowed the aggressiveness that would characterize his entire Civil War career. It seems that an unwritten truce existed which permitted the Baltimore and Ohio Railroad to run train loads of coal at peak capacity from the western Virginia coal fields through Harpers Ferry to Washington D.C. Jackson quickly devised a clever ruse to put the railroad out of commission. He complained to the railroad's management that the continual noise of the trains disturbed his men at rest in their camps at Harpers Ferry. Would the railroad be so kind, he requested, to limit its use of the Harpers Ferry tracks to the two hours between 1100 and 1300?

The railroad's owners, like good gentlemen, complied, perhaps out of fear that Jackson might burn the Harpers Ferry bridge or something drastic like that if they did not comply. The wily Jackson had another plan in mind. He noted that the railroad was as busy as it could be every day from 1100 to 1300. One day he struck. At 1100 he barricaded the eastbound track at Point of Rocks, Maryland (11 miles east of Harpers Ferry) and the west bound track at Martinsburg (18 miles west of Harpers Ferry). Then at 1300 he ordered the tracks to be torn up at both barricades. This clever move stranded more than 400 locomotives and train cars, a prize catch that dealt a crippling loss to the railroad.

Jackson's intense respect for rules and regulations was made clear a short while later. On 24 May, Brig. Gen. Joseph E. Johnston arrived at Harpers Ferry to take command of the district in place of Jackson. Jackson did not doubt Johnston's mission, but he refused to yield command because he had not been notified of it through proper channels. Johnston averted what might have become a very awkward and nasty situation by showing Jackson a letter that outlined his assignment. Johnston did not hold a grudge for the incident, but increased his respect for Jackson. Indeed, Johnston soon gave Jackson command of the best and biggest brigade at Winchester, the future "Stonewall Brigade."

Jackson's first campaign under Johnston was far from pleasant. When Union forces began moving against Harpers Ferry in mid-June, Johnston chose to retreat to Winchester instead of fight. On 15 June 1861 the great Baltimore and Ohio railroad bridges at Harpers Ferry were destroyed, as were most of the rail cars Jackson had captured only a few weeks before. The sight of his "loot" burning must have rankled Jackson as much as Johnston's failure to fight for Harpers Ferry.

Johnston's army then skirmished with Union Maj. Gen. Robert Patterson's army for a month. There were no decisive actions, yet Confederate activity was enough to convince Patterson that the Rebels were preparing to assault him. Johnston seized the opportunity. Leaving a small covering force to face Patterson, on 18 July he took most of his army (including Jackson's brigade) and boarded trains for Manassas Junction, where Gen. P.G.T. Beauregard's Confederate army was being threatened by Brig. Gen. Irvin McDowell's much larger Union *Army of Virginia*. Jackson and his men would earn their treasured nickname of "Stonewall" in the battle of 21 July, First Bull Run.

The Stonewall Brigade

The Stonewall Brigade was probably the single most famous unit in the Confederate Army, being the only brigade to have its nickname sanctioned by the Confederate Congress, (30 May 1863). It consisted of five Virginia infantry regiments (the 2nd, 4th, 5th, 27th, and 33rd) that were raised in the 18 counties which lay in the Shenandoah Valley; the Rockbridge Artillery was also a part of the brigade until October 1862. When first organized in the spring of 1861, the brigade seemed to offer no more promise than any of the others being created at the time. The brigade's morale may have been helped by the fact that all its men came from the same district of Virginia, but what really forged the brigade's unity was the long and hard

training it received from Jackson both before and after First Bull Run. Jackson took command of the brigade in May of 1861, and immediately asserted his control by limiting passes for the men to see their families and installing guards to keep the soldiers in camp. Then constant drill and strict discipline shaped the men into the efficient fighting machine that Jackson wanted and demanded.

Jackson and his brigade arrived at Manassas, Virginia, with Joe Johnston's army just in time to help Beauregard's army defeat Irvin McDowell's attacking Union force. At the opening of the battle of First Bull Run, Jackson was stationed on the Confederate right wing, but he was shifted to the left in order to meet McDowell's flank attack. When Jackson arrived on Henry House Hill, things were not going well for the Confederates. Several brigades had been crushed on Matthews' Hill, and the remaining men were streaming back over Jacksori's position. Undaunted, Jackson, who had suffered a slight hand wound, held his men in line in a woods on the edge of the hill. Though this was the first battle for most of his men, Jackson was able to hold them until just the right moment. Confederate Brig. Gen. Bernard E. Bee saw this, and gave Jackson and his brigade their immortal nickname by shouting, "Look at Jackson's Brigade, it stands like a stone wall! Rally behind the Virginians!" [There has been some discussion that perhaps Bee's remark was criticizing Jackson for sitting still and doing nothing while Bee's men were being overwhelmed. We cannot know Bee's intentions because he was mortally wounded soon after he uttered the famous words.]

Jackson had such regard for the brigade that he requested it be transferred to him when he was given command of the Valley district on 5 November. The brigade served him well as it marched up and down the Valley and fought desperately whenever called upon, particularly at Kernstown and Port Republic. After the Valley Campaign, the brigade continued to be one of Lee's crack units, ranking at the top, along with Hood's Texas Brigade. At Gaines' Mill (27 June 1862), the Stonewall Brigade helped break the Union line in bloody frontal attacks. At Groveton (28 August 1862) it fought the Yankees' best outfit the, Iron Brigade, to a stand-still. Perhaps the

Stonewall Brigade's sternest test was at Antietam (17 September 1862), where it was worn to a frazzle while helping to hold Lee's left wing at the West Woods. The brigade then fought at Fredericksburg, and participated in Jackson's successful flank attack on 2 May 1863 at Chancellorsville. Another successful flank attack came at Stephenson's Depot (15 June 1863), where the brigade captured six enemy regiments. The unit did well at Gettysburg, but was positioned on Culp's Hill, away from the main action of the battle. The next spring it fought at the Wilderness and then met disaster at Spotsylvania, where most of Ed Johnson's division was captured at the Bloody Angle. After this catastrophe only 200 men were left in the brigade, and it had to be consolidated into one regiment. As such it took part in Early's Valley campaign, Monocacy, and the attack on Washington. It then went to the Petersburg trenches. Only 210 men remained in the once proud Stonewall Brigade at the time of Lee's surrender at Appomattox.

The Stonewall Brigade enjoyed its success partly because of its series of distinguished commanders. Stonewall Jackson, who took command on May 1861, was succeeded by Dick Garnett on 14 November 1861. Garnett, who was a strict disciplinarian, was at first received coldly by his men. Though he soon earned their respect, he never seemed to be able to satisfy Jackson. Garnett was relieved of command by Jackson on April 1862 for withdrawing the brigade without orders at Kernstown.

Charles Winder, Garnett's successor, was transferred to the brigade from the 6th South Carolina. He was one of the war's best brigade commanders until he was killed by an artillery shell at Cedar Mountain on 9 August 1862.

Colonel W.H.S. Baylor of the 5th Virginia was acting commander of the Stonewall Brigade until his death at Second Bull Run, after which the brigade was led by Lieutenant Col. Andrew J. Grigsby at Antietam. Due to heavy losses Grigsby was commanding Jackson's division at the end of the battle and Maj. H. J. Williams of the 5th Virginia led the Stonewall Brigade.

For some reason Jackson did not like Grigsby, and had Col. Elisha F. Paxton of the 27th Virginia put in command of the brigade. Paxton served until he was killed at Chancellorsville on 2 May 1863, the same day that Jackson was mortally wounded. Paxton's successor was Col. James A. Walker of the 4th Virginia. Walker was a stern disciplinarian who did not enjoy immediate popularity with his men. He led the brigade for almost a year, until he was wounded and captured at Spotsylvania, the battle that destroyed the brigade.

Jackson was justifiably proud of his brigade, though he did not often reveal his feelings to its men, beyond his congratulatory orders after battles. His true sentiments were expressed when he was in his sick bed after his wound at Chancellorsville. Upon hearing that Jeb Stuart, his temporary replacement as II Corps commander, had urged his troops forward with the cry "Remember Stonewall Jackson!" Jackson said, "The men of the Brigade will be, some day, proud to say to their children, 'I was one of the Stonewall Brigade.' The name 'Stonewall' ought to be attached wholly to the men of the Brigade, and not to me; for it was their steadfast heroism which earned it at First Manassas."

CHAPTER II

The Kernstown Operation

12–23 March 1862

Banks' troops occupied Winchester early on 12 March, and began a casual pursuit of the Confederate column. Turner Ashby, Jackson's bold cavalry commander, had little difficulty keeping the Federals at arm's length. Rumor had it that Ashby had been the last Confederate to leave Winchester on the morning of the 12th. On his way out of town he was intercepted by two mounted Yankees. Ashby supposedly shot one dead and dragged the other away with him as his prisoner.

Jackson reached Strasburg, 18 miles south of Winchester, late on the 12th. Because of Banks' leisurely pursuit, the Confederates remained at Strasburg until the 15th. They then withdrew another 24 miles to Mt. Jackson, which was occupied on the 20th. For the time being the Yankees proceeded no farther south than Strasburg. Banks had no desire or need to press Jackson closely, and was much more interested in stabilizing this front so that he could take the bulk of his corps to join McClellan's drive on Richmond. His exact orders from McClellan, dated 16 March, directed him to move to Manassas, leaving only a reinforced brigade at Front Royal and Strasburg. However, Banks for the moment would not be joining McClellan at Richmond, but would be held back to cover the Potomac line and Washington.

In accordance with these directions, Banks recalled Shields' division from Strasburg and began preparations to dispatch

Major General George B. McClellan's grand plan to capture Richmond was upset by Jackson's unexpected aggressiveness in the Shenandoah Valley.

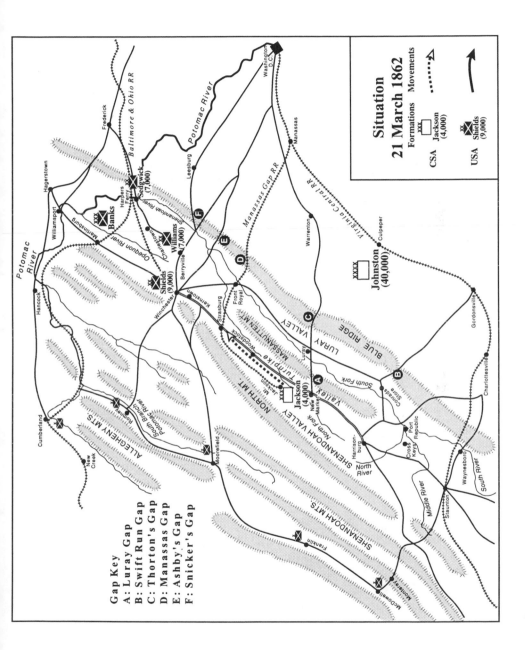

Gap Key
A: Luray Gap
B: Swift Run Gap
C: Thorton's Gap
D: Manassas Gap
E: Ashby's Gap
F: Snicker's Gap

Situation
21 March 1862

Williams' division to Manassas. He had seen no aggressive moves from Jackson, and was aware of the small size of Stonewall's army. Thus it appeared that the front was stabilized and it was safe to withdraw to Winchester in preparation for proceeding to Manassas.

Banks totally misunderstood Jackson's character. Ever since he abandoned Winchester, Jackson had been hankering to strike back at the Yankees. When Ashby reported on the 21st that the enemy had withdrawn from Strasburg, Jackson reacted decisively. He ordered all his infantry to hurry immediately to Strasburg; his entire force was gathered there by the evening of the 22nd, some units having marched 25 miles that day.

Meanwhile, Ashby had kept in close contact with Banks' rear guard. On the evening of 22 March, he skirmished with Banks' pickets a mile south of Winchester and drove them back to the town. This pressure so annoyed Banks that he sent a reinforced infantry brigade to face Ashby. Since Ashby had only three cannons and no more than 300 men, he had little choice but to retire on Kernstown.

The results of Ashby's skirmish were deceiving to both sides. Ashby's aggressiveness convinced Banks that a strong enemy force was nearby. To meet it, he held all of Brig. Gen. James Shields' *2nd Division* in readiness to defend Winchester; Banks' other division, Brig. Gen. Alpheus Williams' *1st*, had left Winchester for Manassas on the morning of the 22nd. On the Confederate side, Ashby in his zeal convinced Jackson that only a small Federal force was screening Winchester. With his typical aggressiveness, Jackson determined to attack the enemy on 23 March, even though it was the Sabbath, a day Jackson normally held too sacred for such activity.

Though the Federals formed to received an attack late on the 22nd, they were not really expecting one. After all, Shields had about 7000 men, at least 50 percent more than the Rebel army was thought to number. Shields sent Col. Nathan Kimball's *1st Brigade*, with one battery, down the Valley Turnpike to a position about midway between Winchester and Kernstown, Col. Jeremiah C. Sullivan's *2nd Brigade* was posted in support of Kimball, with Col. Erastus Tyler's *3rd Brigade* and the cavalry in reserve

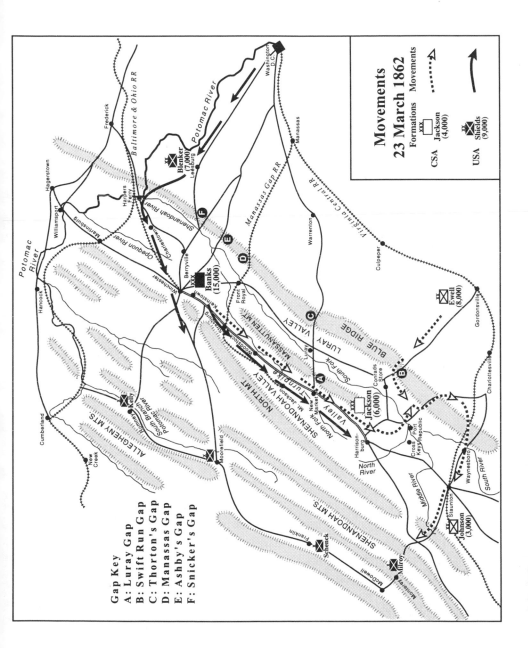

Union troops occupy Winchester following the Confederate evacuation by Jackson's forces.

near the toll gate at the intersection of the Cedar Creek Turnpike and the Valley Turnpike.

Since all seemed secure, Banks himself departed for Washington early on the 23rd. Brigadier General Shields was left in charge at Winchester, though he had been slightly wounded by a shell on the evening of the 22nd. This wound would prevent Shields from taking the field on the 23rd, and the coming battle would be managed in his absence by his senior brigade commander, Col. Nathan Kimball.

The situation on the morning of 23 March 1862 was reported later in these words by General Shields: "Not being able to reconnoiter the front in person, I despatched an experienced

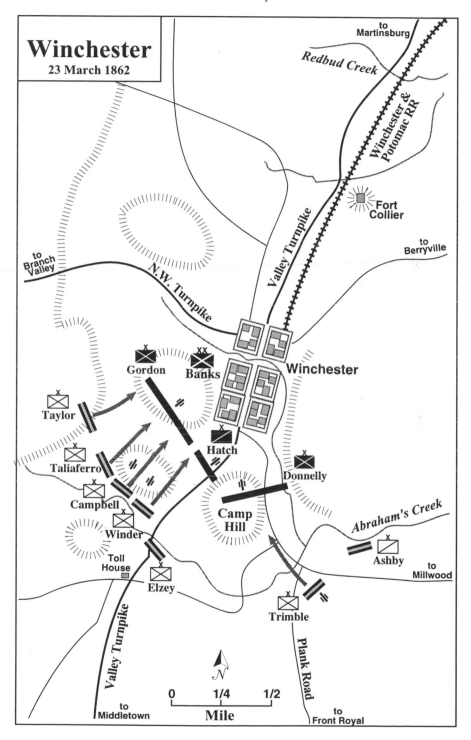

Winchester
23 March 1862

to
Martinsburg

Redbud Creek

Winchester &
Potomac RR

Fort
Collier

to
Branch
Valley

to
Berryville

N.W. Turnpike

Valley Turnpike

Gordon

Banks

Winchester

Taylor

Hatch

Taliaferro

Donnelly

Campbell

Abraham's Creek

Winder

Camp
Hill

Toll
House

Ashby

to
Millwood

Elzey

Trimble

Valley Turnpike

Plank Road

N

0   1/4   1/2
Mile

to
Middletown

to
Front Royal

43

The highlight of Brig. Gen. James Shields' military career was when his troops defeated Jackson's at Kernstown. He often boasted of the victory later, though he had not been on the field because of an earlier wound.

officer, Col. J.T. Mason, of the Fourth Ohio Volunteers, about 9 o'clock A.M., to the front to perform that duty, and to report to me as promptly as possible every circumstance that might indicate the presence of the enemy. About an hour after, Colonel Mason returned, and reported to me that he had carefully reconnoitered the country in front and on both flanks, and found no indications of any hostile force, except that of Ashby. I communicated this information to Maj. Gen. Banks, who was then with me, and, after consulting together, we both concluded that Jackson could not be tempted to hazard himself so far away from his main support. Having both come to this conclusion, Gen. Banks took his departure for Washington, being already under orders to that effect. The officers of his staff, however, remained behind, intending to leave for Centreville in the afternoon."

At dawn on the 23rd Jackson rushed forward four companies of the Stonewall Brigade under Capt. J.Q.A. Nadenbousch of the 2nd Virginia to support Ashby, and then began moving forward the rest of his command. Because they had 14 miles to cover to reach Kernstown, Nadenbousch's men did not reach Ashby

Colonel Nathan Kimball, commander of Shields' First Brigade at Kernstown. Because Shields was wounded the day before the battle, it was Kimball who led the Union troops to victory.

until 1000 hours. By then a heavy skirmish was going on about a mile north of Kernstown. Nadenbousch's arrival almost doubled Ashby's strength (he actually had no more than 300 cavalrymen on the field that day), but Ashby soon decided he had to retreat because of the heavy enemy columns approaching from the north. Ashby's withdrawal to a new line immediately south of Kernstown had a key effect on the future course of the battle—it left open Pritchard's Hill, a low ridge west of the Valley Turnpike that dominated the entire area from Kernstown to the Middle Road. Seeing Ashby retire, Colonel Kimball promptly ordered Sullivan's brigade and a battery to occupy Pritchard's Hill.

Jackson's main force began reaching Kernstown around 1300. Jackson was aware that his troops were exhausted from two days of hard marching-they had marched 22 miles from Mount Jackson to Strasburg on the 22nd and another 14 miles on the 23rd to reach Kernstown. He later claimed that he was ready to go into camp at that moment and fight the next day, but then he

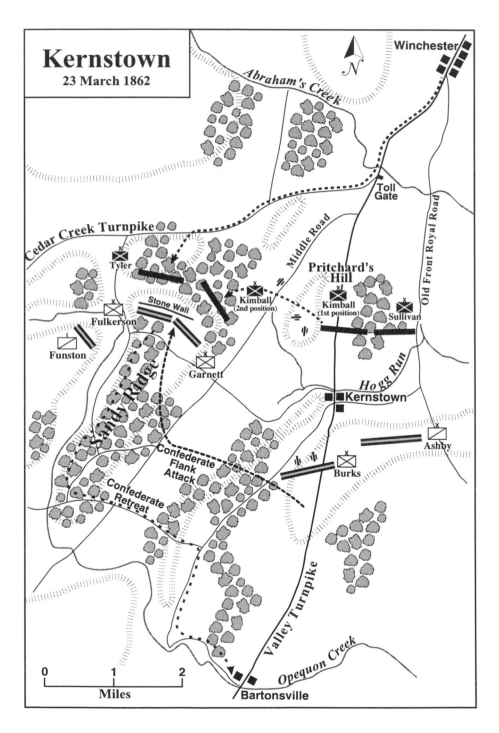

Kernstown
23 March 1862

Winchester

Abraham's Creek

N

Toll Gate

Cedar Creek Turnpike

Middle Road

Old Front Royal Road

Tyler

Pritchard's Hill

Kimball
(2nd position)

Kimball
(1st position)

Sullivan

Stone Wall

Fulkerson

Garnett

Funston

Sandy Ridge

Hogg Run

Kernstown

Ashby

Confederate Flank Attack

Burks

Confederate Retreat

Valley Turnpike

Opequon Creek

0   1   2
Miles

Bartonsville

The stone wall at Kernstown which was the center of the battle, as seen from the Confederate side.

changed his mind: "Though it was very desirable to prevent the enemy from leaving the Valley, yet I deemed it best not to attack until morning. But subsequently, ascertaining that the Federals had a position from which our forces could be seen, I concluded that it would be dangerous to postpone the attack until the next day, as reinforcements might be brought up during the night."

What probably helped change Jackson's mind was the fact that the Union position on Pritchard's Hill, though strong, did not appear to be heavily defended, and the entire Union line seemed vulnerable to a flank attack from the west. Here a long wooded ridge ran on the western side of Opequon Creek, parallel to and about two miles east of the Valley Pike. Jackson decided to leave Col. Jesse S. Burks' brigade and part of Ashby's cavalry, altogether about one-third of his force, to face the Union troops on Pritchard's Hill, while he sent Col. Samuel V. Fulkerson's small brigade with Garnett's Stonewall Brigade to turn the Federal right. The plan seemed a reasonable one, but did not take into account the weary state of Jackson's infantry. In addition, straggling had reduced his brigades to a strength of 3000.

Another weakness of Jackson's plan was the fact that his key attack on the left was not spearheaded by the crack Stonewall Brigade, but by Fulkerson's small brigade of only two regiments (23rd and 47th Virginia; his 48th Virginia was absent guarding the supply trains). The final and most notable weakness of Jackson's plan was the fact that he did not know for certain the enemy's total strength or disposition. Kimball had taken care to keep many of his troops out of Ashby's view, and Jackson was consequently unaware that he was outnumbered on the field more than two to one.

At about 1530 Jackson began his movement against the Federal right. From the beginning things did not go well. As Fulkerson's brigade crossed the fields west of Kernstown, the Confederates fell under the fire of the Federal guns on Pritchard's Hill—a fire "that might well have made veterans quail," Fulkerson later wrote. Fulkerson was happy to reach the cover of the timber on the ridge that was his goal, and he began forming battle line behind a stone wall that crossed the width of the ridge. Fulkerson was then surprised to see two regiments of the enemy approaching his line. Colonel Kimball had anticipated Jackson's flanking move and sent Tyler's *3rd Brigade* to his right as a precaution. Tyler arrived only minutes after Fulkerson had taken position, and the battle soon spread up and down Fulkerson's stone wall.

Fulkerson at first had no difficulty repulsing the two regiments that formed Tyler's vanguard. But when the rest of Tyler's regiments came up, firing grew heavier and Fulkerson realized that he would not be able to attack until his supports— the Stonewall Brigade—came up.

Brig. Gen. Richard Garnett, commander of the Stonewall Brigade, was having difficulty getting his command forward. His strength had already been diminished when his largest regiment, the 5th Virginia, was kept behind by Jackson as a reserve. He then received what he thought was an order from Jackson to send only the 33rd Virginia forward to Fulkerson. As the 33rd advanced, Jackson was furious to find the remainder of the Stonewall Brigade inactive, and he began leading the regiments forward himself. This led to great confusion as the commanders of the 2nd, 4th and 27th Virginia regiments began

Brig. Gen. Richard Garnett led the Stonewall Brigade into action at Kernstown. After conditions forced him to retreat without Jackson's assent, Stonewall had him arrested. He was later transferred to Pickett's division and was killed in action at Gettysburg. (This portrait may actually be of his cousin, Robert S. Garnett).

receiving orders from both Garnett and Jackson. Meanwhile Garnett, who had already reached Fulkerson's line, grew concerned about the confusion in his brigade and made preparations to pull back the 33rd Virginia until the situation became clearer. He had no idea what Jackson's battle plan was, even though he was technically Jackson's second-in-command, and he was genuinely concerned that his brigade's confusion possibly stemmed from a new order from Jackson that had not reached him where he was on the front line.

It was well after 1600 before the Stonewall Brigade was reunited and formed on Fulkerson's right behind the stone wall that traversed the ridge. For a while the reinforced Confederate line held off Tyler's Union 3rd Brigade. At one point the 37th Virginia of Fulkerson's brigade, which held the far right of the Confederate line, rushed across a field racing a Federal regiment for a stone wall at the center of the field. The Confederates won the race and blasted the Yankees in the face. Twice Tyler tried to turn Fulkerson's left, but failed. The heat of the conflict then focused on the Stonewall Brigade. Here the Federals began gaining the upper hand as Kimball began switching regiments from his unengaged left to join the heavy fight on the right.

By now it was very clear to Jackson that the battle was not progressing as he had planned. The severity of the fighting on the left made it obvious that the size of the Union army on the field was much greater than he had thought. At one point Jackson sent Sandie Pendleton to examine the strength and position of the Union army. When Pendleton reported that the Union force was at least 10,000, Jackson realized what deep trouble he was in. His immediate reply was only, "Say nothing of it, we are in for it."

Jackson understood that there was no longer any chance of winning a victory—he would be hard pressed simply to extricate his battle weary command from the field. Accordingly, he sent the 5th Virginia forward to join Garnett, and ordered the 48th Virginia to hurry forward from the trains it had been guarding south of Kernstown. He also shifted the 42nd Virginia from Burks' brigade over to the left. Burks' other regiments, the 21st Virginia and 1st Virginia Battalion, had already been sent to reinforce Garnett; this left only a few of Ashby's cavalry and a handful of cannons to hold the right and the army's retreat route along the Valley Turnpike.

While Jackson was rushing the 5th Virginia and other reserves to his hard pressed left, Garnett was facing an immensely difficult situation. His men had been fighting for two hours against a superior force of the enemy and were now exhausted, disorganized, and running out of ammunition. Faced with the prospect of being overwhelmed or outflanked, Garnett at about 1800 gave the command for the Stonewall Brigade to begin withdrawing. His decision to retreat was probably a sound one, but it was audacious because it was not ordered or approved by Jackson. In addition, Garnett's withdrawal exposed Fulkerson's brigade to isolation and possible destruction or capture.

It was not long before Garnett's withdrawal turned into a rout. Jackson was furious to see his pet brigade fleeing in disgrace. Had it not been for a bold front put forward by the 5th Virginia, Jackson's whole army might have been lost. Though badly outnumbered and outflanked, the 5th formed on a small hill and delayed the advancing Northern regiments a precious few minutes until it was reinforced by the 42nd Virginia and a few cannons. This makeshift line delayed the Federals another 15 minutes until it was forced to yield. The 5th and 42nd then joined the Confederate retreat to the south, shielded from the Union pursuit by a small cavalry detachment. The coming of darkness then brought an end to the day's combat.

The battle had been a harsh one for the Confederates. Jackson's small force lost 455 men killed and wounded and 263 captured, about one-fourth of the number engaged-the highest percentage loss for the Southerners in any battle up to that time. They also lost two cannons, but no flags. Union losses were 103 killed, 441 wounded, and 24 missing.

There is no question that Jackson suffered defeat at the battle of Kernstown. Indeed, General Shields later boasted that he was the only commander to defeat Jackson in the war, though he had spent the entire battle in bed because of his wound and the Union army on the field had been commanded by Col. Nathan Kimball. Jackson had failed in his effort to retake Winchester largely because of his misunderstanding of the size and strength of the Union force there. He was aware that most of the Union troops in the Valley had departed to the east, but he was not certain exactly what forces remained behind. Shields had taken care to keep most of his 10,000–man division concealed from Confederate view before the battle, and had no trouble convincing Turner Ashby that there were only a few Yankee regiments in the area. Ashby's report of this apparent situation gave Jackson the impetus to make an attack that was bold under any conditions. His misunderstanding of the size of the Union army also led him to make the tactical mistake of ordering a flank attack against the enemy line before first reconnoitering the ground. Jackson thought that the entire Union force was in sight on Pritchard's Hill, and he did not handle his flank attack as skillfully as he might have. He was particularly at fault in the confusing orders he gave to Garnett and then to Garnett's regiments individually without following the chain of command.

All in all, however, Jackson did a creditable job at Kernstown considering the number of troops he had available. A more

Stonewall Jackson's staff. Clockwise from 0100: Maj. Robert L. Dabney, AAG; Lt. Col. Wallan, Chief of Ordnance; Lt. Col. Sandie Pendleton, AAG; Capt. J. G. Morrison, aide; Maj. D. B. Bridgeford, Quartermaster; Maj. Henry Kyd Douglas; Capt. J. Smith, aide; Maj. Hunter McGuire, Medical Director; Capt. Jed Hotchkiss, Topographical Engineer; Maj. Wells J. Hawks, Chief of Commissary.

*Union Colonel Erastus B. Tyler leads his **Third Brigade** in a charge against Jackson's troops at Kernstown. The battle was a decisive setback for Jackson, who unsuccessfully attempted to defeat a larger Union army.*

aggressive Union commander would have made an effort to smash Jackson's right wing and take control of the Valley Turnpike after Jackson began stripping his right to reinforce his hard pressed left. But it seems that Jackson's boldness and aggressiveness convinced Shields and Kimball that the Confederates had from 11,000 to 15,000 men, two to three times their actual strength. Why else would Jackson have attacked a full Union division of 10,000? All things considered, Jackson was lucky to have done as well as he did and then escape with his army relatively intact.

Though Kernstown was a tactical defeat, it turned out to be a strategic victory for the Confederates. Jackson's orders had been to watch Johnston's far left flank and keep Banks from reinforcing McClellan. When he heard of Jackson's attack at Kernstown, McClellan figured that Jackson had been reinforced, and ordered Alpheus Williams' division, which had left Winchester the day before the battle of Kernstown, to return to the Valley. Banks, who had left Winchester on the day of Kernstown, promptly returned to his command. He then received new orders to "push Jackson hard and drive him well beyond Strasburg, pursuing at least as far as Woodstock, and, if possible, with cavalry to Mount Jackson."

Jackson was well aware of the results he had achieved at Kernstown—in his battle report written over two weeks afterwards he wrote: "Though Winchester was not recovered, yet the more important object for the present, that of calling back troops that were leaving the valley, and thus preventing a junction of Banks' command with other forces, was accomplished, in addition to his heavy loss in killed and wounded. Under these circumstances I feel justified in saying that, though the field is in possession of the enemy, yet the essential fruits of the battle are ours." Jackson's troops also felt good, in spite of their defeat. Stonewall wrote his wife on 28 March: "My little army is in excellent spirits. It feels that it inflicted a severe blow upon the enemy." Nor did the efforts of Jackson and his men go unrecognized by the Confederate Congress, which soon after the battle resolved "That the thanks of Congress are due, and they are hereby tendered, to Maj. Gen. T.J. Jackson and the officers and men under his command for their gallant and meritorious service in the successful engagement with a greatly superior force of the enemy, near Kernstown, Frederick County, Virginia, on the 23rd day of March, 1862."

Young Stonewall

Thomas J. Jackson was born at Clarksburg in West Virginia on 21 January 1824. His family was of Scotch-Irish lineage and had been settled in western Virginia since about 1750. Various ancestors had served in civil and military posts in the Colonial period, the Revolution, the early years of the Republic, and the War of 1812. One of four children, Thomas' father died when he was three, leaving the family destitute. His mother—to whom he remained very devoted—remarried but died in childbirth when Thomas was seven. Thomas and his siblings then lived with various relatives, including an uncle who was particularly fond of the young boy. By the time he reached adulthood—only Thomas and his sister Laura survived to see 21—Thomas had acquired a rudimentary education and had worked in a variety of jobs. After his uncle died during the California gold rush, Thomas decided to apply to West Point.

Thomas had actively pursued his West Point appointment. When he heard that a cadet from his congressional district had resigned soon after entry, Thomas sought the support of his most influential relatives and went personally to see his congressman, Samuel Hays, in Washington. Hays was concerned about Thomas' lack of formal education, and arranged an interview with the Secretary of War. Here Jackson's determination won the day, and the Secretary approved the appointment, saying, "Sir, you have a good name. Go to West Point, and the first man who insults you knock him down, and have it charged to my account!"

Jackson soon felt his lack of academic background for a program difficult as West Point's. He was not a quick learner, but worked hard and retained well what he studied. As he himself put it, he "studied very hard" for what he got at West Point. A classmate said of him, "He had a rough time in the Academy at first, for his want of previous training placed him at a great disadvantage, and it was all he could do to pass his first examination. We were studying algebra, and maybe analytical geometry, that winter, and Jackson was very low in class standing. All lights were put out at 'taps,' and just before the signal he would pile up his grate with anthracite coal, and lying prone before it on the floor, would work away at his lessons by the glare of the fire, which scorched his very brain, till a late hour of the night. This evident determination to succeed not only aided his efforts directly, but impressed his instructors in his favor, and he rose steadily year by year, till we used to say: 'If we had to stay here another year, Old Jack would be at the head of the class.'"

Jackson's behavior at West Point was exemplary. He picked up only a few demerits, and generally kept to himself, having but few close friends. He matured in body as well as mind while attending the Academy. His frame filled out, and his performance and confidence in his work improved yearly. He fully expected to be expelled after his first year, but ended up ranking 17th in a class of 70 when he graduated in 1846. His class included such future notables as generals McClellan, Foster, Reno, Stoneman, Couch, and Gibbon of the Union army; and generals A. P. Hill, Pickett, Maury, D. R. Jones, W. D. Smith, and Wilcox of the Confederate army.

Jackson graduated from West Point at the beginning of the war with Mexico, and immediately entered the action. As a lieutenant in the 1st Artillery, he fought in almost every battle from Vera Cruz to the fall of Mexico City. So eager was he for advancement that he sought and received an appointment to the battery of the aggressive Capt. John B. Magruder. Jackson soon rose to be Magruder's second-in-command, and won the rank of brevet captain for his gallantry at Cherubusco on 20 August 1847. At Chapultepec on 13 September, Jackson's handling of himself and his section under fire won the praise of Magruder and Generals Scott, Pillow, and Worth. One of his friends described the scene as follows: 'Lieutenant Jackson's section of Magruder's battery was subjected to plunging fire from the Castle of Chapultepec. The little six-pounders could effect nothing against the guns of the Mexicans, of much heavier caliber, firing from an elevation. The horses were killed or disabled, and the men became so demoralized that they deserted the guns and sought shelter behind a wall or embankment. Lieutenant Jackson remained at the guns, walking back and forth, and kept saying, 'See, there is not danger; I am not hit!' While standing with his legs wide apart, a cannonball passed between them . . . . This bravery earned him a promotion to brevet major.

When the fighting ended, garrison life in Mexico City enthralled the new major. After great pains he learned to speak Spanish, and he also developed a zest for dancing. But the greatest event of his sojourn in Mexico was his introduction to the Episcopal religion by Col. Francis Taylor, commander of the 1st Artillery Regiment.

After the Mexican War Jackson did garrison duty in New York and Florida for a time, before accepting a post at V.M.I.

Jackson's Lieutenants

Stonewall Jackson was generally well served by most of his subordinates during the Valley Campaign. He was, of course, fortunate in having unity of command. Moreover, Jackson's command structure was much more streamlined, more efficient, and more flexible than that of his opponents, particularly Frémont. For ease of control, Stonewall retained direct command of his own division. This probably increased the work load of his staff, but usually made little difference in field operations. Jackson was always with his troops and often shuffled brigades with Dick Ewell, commander of his other division.

Maj. Gen. Richard S. Ewell (1817-1872) was one of Jackson's most talented subordinates. Like so many other Confederate officers, Ewell's prewar career included West Point (1840) and service in the Mexican and Indian Wars. He commanded a brigade at First Bull Run, and in January 1862 was promoted to major general. "Old Baldy" led a division under Jackson in the Valley Campaign, the Seven Days' Battles, and the Second Bull Run Campaign. He was a topnotch fighter whose abilities were well respected by Jackson, though Ewell's sharp tongue, salty language, and nasty disposition were a far cry from Stonewall's temperament.

Ewell's last battle with Stonewall was Groveton (28 August 1862), where he lost his left leg. When he returned to duty nine months later, Jackson was dead. Ewell, now equipped with a wooden leg, found himself in the unenviable job of trying to fill Jackson's shoes as commander of Lee's II Corps. By his performance at Gettysburg, Ewell showed that he was not up to commanding a unit as large as a corps; his indecision on the evening of 1 July canceled what could have been a timely attack on the Union lines on Cemetery Hill, and his poor timing on 2 and 3 July undermined Lee's master battle plan.

Ewell continued in corps command until the spring of 1864. During the battle of Spotsylvania he fell off his horse (he needed to be strapped on because of his wooden leg) and was unable to continue in field command. He was then assigned to command the defenses of Richmond. This job promised relative inactivity, but the position became critical when Grant attacked the Confederate capital in the summer of 1864. Ewell remained at his post until the city fell on 3 April 1865. During the retreat from Richmond he was captured on 6 April at Sayler's Creek. Because of his rank and reputation, he was not paroled until 19 August 1865.

Brig. Gen. Edward "Allegheny" Johnson (1816-1873) was another of the able subordinates who helped Jackson attain victory during the Valley Campaign. Like so many of his brother Confederate generals, Johnson was a West Point graduate (1830) with experience in the Seminole War, the Mexican War, and western garrison duty. When the Civil War broke out, he resigned from the U.S. Army to become colonel of the 12th Virginia. In December 1861 he was appointed a brigadier general in charge of a reinforced brigade near Staunton in the upper Shenandoah Valley. In early May 1862 he combined forces with Jackson to win the battle of McDowell, where he was wounded in the foot.

Johnson's foot wound did not heal properly and forced him to remain inactive for almost a year. In February 1863 he returned to duty with the rank of major general. He then commanded Jackson's old division at Gettysburg, the Wilderness, and Spotsylvania. Johnson was among the prisoners when his division was shattered at Spotsylvania's Bloody Angle on the morning of 12 May 1864. After being exchanged, he led a division in Hood's army during the disastrous Tennessee campaign of late 1864. Johnson's second capture at the battle of Nashville put him out of the war for good.

Brig. Gen. William Wing Loring (1818-1886) had a distinguished Civil War career that was overshadowed by his inability shared with several other generals-to get along with Stonewall Jackson. His prewar career included experience in the Seminole War and the Mexican War, where he lost an arm at Chapultepec. He also commanded the Department of Oregon (1849-1851) and then the Department of New Mexico (1860-1861), besides playing key roles in several Indian campaigns and the Mormon expedition. When the Civil War broke out, he sided with Virginia, though he did not believe in secession per se. After being appointed a brigadier general, he served in Lee's abortive Cheat Mountain campaign. In early 1862 he was placed in command of the so-called Army of Southwestern Virginia.

Loring's conflict with Jackson began in mid-January 1862 when Stonewall captured Romney. Jackson directed Loring to occupy the town, but Loring had no desire to do so. Loring immediately went over Jackson's head and complained to Secretary of War Judah P. Benjamin about being posted in such an isolated and vulnerable position. When Benjamin ordered Jackson to recall Loring's command to Winchester, Jackson was furious. There was no way he was going to tolerate such insubordination, and on 31 January he wrote to Benjamin threatening to resign.

Fortunately for the Confederacy, Jackson also complained to John Letcher, Governor of Virginia, about what had happened. Letcher sided with Jackson and gave Secretary Benjamin a heated lesson in military etiquette. The end result was that Jackson stayed in command and Loring was transferred to the West.

Loring was assigned to division command in the Army of Mississippi. There he played a controversial role at the battle of Champion Hill on 16 May 1863. Through incompetency or misunderstanding of orders, Loring failed to hold a key position and was blamed by some for the loss of the battle, which opened the way for Grant to attack Vicksburg. In the confusion following Champion Hill, Loring and his men were unable to withdraw to Vicksburg and so were not involved in the battle or surrender there.

Despite his track record, Loring rose still higher in rank and responsibility. He commanded a corps at Atlanta, and was Hood's second-in-command at Franklin and Nashville. He then served with Joe Johnston's army in North Carolina until the close of the war.

Following the war, Loring served abroad as a mercenary general, as did several other former Confederate generals of note. In 1869 he accepted an appointment as a brigadier general in the army of the Khedive of Egypt. He remained in Egyptian service for 10 years, commanding a division and receiving the title of "Pasha."

Brig. Gen. Richard B. Garnett (1817-1863) was another Confederate general whose career was marred by conflict with Stonewall Jackson. Garnett's prewar military service was extensive. After graduating from West Point in 1841 he fought in the Seminole War, the Mexican War, and the Utah Expedition. He began the Civil War as a major in the Confederate artillery. In November 1861 Garnett was promoted to brigadier general and assigned to command the Stonewall Brigade, succeeding Stonewall himself.

Garnett's new job proved to be filled with pressure. Jackson wanted nothing but strict obedience from his subordinates, particularly the general in charge of his old brigade. At the battle of Kernstown on 25 March 1862 Jackson sent Garnett and the Stonewall Brigade to attack the Union right. Garnett ran into much more opposition than Jackson expected, and was not able to accomplish his mission. In fact, the brigade began to run out of ammunition and was on the verge of breaking up. Garnett accepted responsibility to disengage and withdraw. This move saved the brigade but earned Jackson's deep animosity. Jackson relieved Garnett from command and put him on trial for disobedience of orders. The case was not permitted to be heard to completion, however. Evidence was still being heard when Jackson had to break camp to enter the Cedar Mountain campaign in early August.

Garnett's trial was never resumed. To avoid further conflict with Jackson, he was transferred to another command. Garnett led Pickett's old brigade at Antietam, and then became a fixture in Pickett's division in the Fredericksburg and North Carolina campaigns.

Garnett was an excellent fighter, but his career was haunted by Jackson even after Stonewall died as a result of the wounds he received at Chancellorsville. Garnett was not feeling well at Gettysburg, but went into action anyway, no doubt goaded by the stain that Jackson's charges had made on his military re-

cord. He was cut down only a few yards from the stone wall on Cemetery Ridge at Gettysburg, at the height of Pickett's Charge. His body was never identified, and lies now in an unmarked grave at Gettysburg or Richmond.

Jackson's Subordinates. Jackson's army included several minor ranked officers of note. Brig. Gen. Richard Taylor (1826-1879) eventually became a lieutenant general in charge of the Trans Mississippi Department; it was he who defeated Banks in the 1864 Red River Campaign. Brig. Gen. Isaac Trimble (1802-1888, West Point 1822) became a major general and was wounded and captured in Pickett's Charge at Gettysburg. Brig. Gen. William B. Taliaferro (1822-1898) and Arnold Elzey (1816-1871, West Point 1837) also became major generals late in the war, as did Harry Hays (1820-1876), colonel of the 7th Louisiana, who was wounded at Port Republic.

Brig. Gen. Charles S. Winder (1829-1862, West Point 1850) had prewar field experience fighting Indians in the Northwest. When the war began he resigned from the U.S. Army and accepted a commission as major of Confederate artillery. He commanded South Carolina's Arsenal Battery at Fort Sumter and then was appointed colonel of the 6th South Carolina Infantry, which he soon forged into one of the war's best regiments. Winder took command of the Stonewall Brigade on 2 April 1862 as successor to Richard B. Garnett, the popular commander whom Stonewall Jackson court-martialed for his conduct at Kernstown. Jackson's action was so unpopular with the men of the Stonewall Brigade that they treated Winder with an icy coolness and even rudeness. Winder would have nothing of this sort of treatment and promptly put an end to it. He called in the colonels of the offending regiments and informed them that he would hold them personally responsible for the behavior of their troops. This put an end to the soldiers' catcalls, but it still took Winder a while to win the affection of his troops. He was an extreme disciplinarian, a trait that pleased Jackson much more than it did the men of the Stone wall Brigade.

After being transferred to the Stonewall Brigade, Winder wasted no time revealing his fighting and administrative strengths. He performed very well in the Valley and Peninsula Campaigns, and rose to command Jackson's old division. He was ill at the battle of Cedar Mountain on 9 August 1862 but insisted

on entering combat anyway, only to have his promising career ended by a cannonball.

Other Confederate brigadiers of note were Turner Ashby, who is dealt with elsewhere, and George "Maryland" Steuart (1828-1903, West Point 1848). Steuart, perhaps because of his Maryland political connections, never rose above the rank of brigadier general, and was still commanding a brigade when he was captured at Spotsylvania in May 1864.

Colonels who commanded brigades in Jackson's force showed less potential. John M. Patton (1826-1898), great-uncle of World War II's George Patton) and William C. Scott (1809-1865) both resigned from the army because of ill health. John Campbell (1823-1886) resigned in October 1862 when he was not promoted to permanent brigade command.

Stonewall's Staff

One of the contributing reasons for Jackson's success in the Valley Campaign was the competent, dedicated, and close knit staff he put together to keep his army running and carry out his instructions.

Jedediah Hotchkiss. One of the key players on Jackson's staff was South's premier map maker, Jed Hotchkiss (1827-1899). Hotchkiss, a native of New York State, was an amateur cartographer who in 1852 founded an academy in the Valley, at Mossy Creek, near Luray. In 1861 he joined the army of the Confederacy and served without distinction

in western Virginia. Hotchkiss' association with Jackson began on 26 March 1862 when he was serving as adjutant of the Augusta County militia. Stonewall asked him to "make me a map of the Valley" from Harpers Ferry to Lexington, and was so satisfied with the result that he retained Hotchkiss on his staff with the rank of major.

After Jackson's death, Hotchkiss continued to serve the commanders of the II Corps as topographical engineer. His most notable service came at Cedar Creek (19 Oct 1864), where his knowledge of the terrain significantly aided the successful Confederate surprise attack at the beginning of the battle.

Following the war, Hotchkiss returned to his teaching career. He also spent a great deal of time and energy working for the Presbyterian Church and for the development of Virginia's natural resources. He is best remembered today for two books he wrote on Virginia in the Civil War, and for contributing many of the Confederate maps that appear in the *Atlas of the Official Records of the Union and Confederate Armies*. Hotchkiss' wartime journals were edited by Archie P. McDonald and published in 1973 under the title *Make Me a Map of the Valley, the Civil War Journal of Stonewall Jackson's Topographer Alexander Swift Pendleton*.

"Sandie" Pendleton (1840-1864), a personal friend of Jackson's, served on Stonewall's staff in several capacities. Pendleton, the son of William N. Pendleton (1809-1883), who was Lee's chief-of-Artillery during the entire war, met Jackson while he was a student at Washington College in Lexington, Virginia, and Stonewall was a professor at nearby V.M.I. The two belonged to the same local literary society, and shared a common religious dedication. When the war broke out, Sandie was commissioned a lieutenant in the Engineers, and was assigned to Jackson's staff in late May of 1861. Two months later he bacame Jackson's ordnance officer. His efficiency and dedication won Jackson's admiration, as did his bravery—at Kernstown he helped man a cannon whose crew had fallen. For these reasons Jackson in the late summer of 1862 reassigned

Pendleton to the important post of assistant adjutant general effectively, chief of stafff the II Corps. In this capacity, Pendleton took care of all of Jackson's paperwork, and even wrote many of Jackson's official battle reports. Jackson particularly valued his clarity of style and knowledge of army detail.

When Jackson died, Pendleton served as one of the pallbearers at his funeral. Jackson's successor, Lieutenant Gen. "Old Baldy" Ewell, elevated Pendleton to the post of chief of staff of the II Corps. Pendleton continued to serve with the corps until he was mortally wounded at Fisher's Hill, Virginia, on 22 September 1864. Sandie Pendleton, the consummate staff officer, was then buried in Lexington cemetery not far from the grave of his mentor and friend, Stonewall Jackson.

Dr. Hunter McGuire (1835-1900), medical director, had a varied education at Winchester Medical College, Jefferson Medical College in Philadelphia, and the Medical College of Virginia at Richmond. When the war began, McGuire enlisted as a private in the 2nd Virginia Infantry of what would become the Stonewall Brigade. He became a surgeon on 4 May 1861, and was promoted to brigade surgeon in June. He showed great industry in his office—he put together a working ambulance corps and established a system of reserve hospitals for Jackson's command. He also got along very well personally with the eccentric Jackson. When Jackson was wounded by his own men at Chancellorsville on the evening of 2 May 1863, it was McGuire who amputated the general's left arm. After

Jackson's death, McGuire rose from medical director of the II Corps to be medical director of Lee's whole army. Following the war, he became a professor at the Virginia Medical College and was an early authority on obstetrics and gynecology. He later helped found the Richmond University College of Medicine and also served as a president of the American Medical Association.

The Rev. Robert Lewis Dabney (1820-1898) was Jackson's assistant adjutant general (chief of staff) during most of the Valley Campaign. Dabney was born in Louisa County, Virginia, and attended Hampden Sidney College, the University of Virginia, and Union Theological Seminary, before becoming a Presbyterian minister. Dabney's appointment as Jackson's A.A.G. in late April 1861 came as a complete surprise to everyone, including Dabney. He had a first class intelligence, but no military experience whatsoever. When he pointed this out, Stonewall replied, "Rest today and study the Articles of War tomorrow." Dabney proved to be an able administrator, and was Jackson's firm friend and messmate. For reasons of ill health he resigned from the army following the Seven Days Battles. After the war, Dabney returned to the Union Theological Seminary. In 1883 he moved to Texas for his health and served as Professor of Philosophy at the University of Texas, until his retirement in 1894. Dabney is best known for his writings, particularly his *Life of Gen. Thomas J. Jackson* (1866).

Col. John T.L. Preston (1811-1870), Jackson's first A.A.G., was one of the founders of V.M.I., and taught there from 1839 to 1882. He began

the war as lieutenant colonel of the 9th Virginia, but because of his pre-war association with Jackson at V.M.I. he became Jackson's A.A.G. on 22 October 1861. Preston and Sandie Pendleton were Jackson's two original staff members when he took command of the Valley army on 30 April 1861. Preston stayed with Jackson only a short while before being ordered back to V.M.I. on 27 December 1861, to be succeeded as Jackson's A.A.G. by Reverend Dabney and then by Sandie Pendleton

Maj. John Harman was noted before the war for running a stage-coach line in the Valley. As such he was a logical choice for quartermaster of the Stonewall Brigade. In November 1861 he tried to resign, but Jackson talked him into staying on as quartermaster of the Valley army. Harman was famous for his foul mouth, an attribute needed by a mule driver but offensive to the pious Jackson. He did a marvelous job of keeping the army's transport together, particularly in the strenuous McDowell campaign. At one point in that campaign Jackson accused Harman of not working hard enough, and Harman responded by resigning. Jackson had the presence of mind to back off and apologize, one of the few times he ever did so to a subordinate. During the drive on Winchester in mid-May Jackson approached Harman angrily because he heard that many wagons were far in the rear due to bad roads; Stonewall was pleased to hear that Harman had doubled the teams in order to keep the ammunition wagons in pace with the army. Harman did a fine job removing the captured stores from Winchester during Jackson's mad rush up the Valley at the end of May. After the war, Harman returned to his stagecoach line, no doubt thankful that he no longer had as stern a boss as Stonewall.

Maj. Wells J. Hawks, who served as Jackson's chief of commissary, had been a successful carriage maker before the war, had served in the Virginia state legislature, and was an officer in the state militia. When the war broke out, he accepted a commission as a captain in the 2nd Virginia, in charge of the regimental commissary. He was later promoted to major to take the same position on Jackson's staff. In that assignment his most famous task was to provide the lemons that Stonewall continually sucked. Where he got them, nobody knew. After Jackson died, Hawks served on the staffs of generals Ewell and Early. During the Gettysburg Campaign he had charge of the money extorted from the Pennsylvania towns, a burden he speedily hustled out of Pennsylvania to Winchester when the Battle of Gettysburg began.

Henry Kyd Douglas (1840-1903), who was handsome, affable, and the youngest member of Jackson's staff, earned his post as an aide to Jackson largely through his friendship with Sandie Pendleton. As a native of Shepherdstown, he was intimately acquainted with the lower Valley and provided invaluable topographical service to Jackson, particularly in the Harpers Ferry and Antietam Campaigns. One of his most arduous missions was a ride he made of 100 miles to take Ewell the orders to join Jackson and help drive Banks from the Valley.

He was directed to deliver the order overnight and did so, fainting from exhaustion immediately thereafter.

Douglas graduated from Franklin and Marshall College in 1859, passed his bar exams in 1860, and practiced law in St. Louis for a year until the war broke out. He first enlisted as a private in the 2nd Virginia Infantry, and soon rose to lieutenant and then captain. On Jackson's staff he served as assistant inspector general and then assistant adjutant general. Later he served as chief of staff for generals Ed Johnson, John Gordon, Jubal Early, J.H. Pegram, and John A. Walker.

Douglas was badly wounded at Gettysburg on 3 July 1863 and carried the bullet for the rest of the war; he was also captured and held prisoner for several months at Johnson's Island in Ohio. Upon returning to service, he joined the staff of Gen. John A. Walker. At Petersburg Douglas was appointed colonel of the consolidated 13th and 49th Virginia Regiments. Later, in the war's last campaign he led the remnants of the old "Light Division," once commanded by A.P. Hill. This command served as the army's rear guard on the last two days of the war, and was the last Confederate infantry brigade to surrender at Appomattox.

Upon the close of the war, Douglas was arrested for having his picture taken in a Confederate uniform, an act that was contrary to Federal military decree. For this offense he was sentenced to imprisonment at Fort Delaware. At this time he also got involved in the Lincoln assassination investigation, perhaps because he was an acquaintance of Mary Surratt, one of the conspirators who was convicted and hanged. Upon release from prison in September 1865, Douglas resumed his law practice. Later he became a judge and served as adjutant general of Maryland from 1892 to 1896. Though handsome, he never married.

Douglas is best remembered as the author of a fine memoir, *I Rode with Stonewall*, in 1863-1866, but never published. Instead, he used his "Stonewall Papers"—as he called them—as the basis for several articles he published. He revised the original manuscript in 1898-1899, but still did not publish it. After his death in 1903 the manuscript was lost for 37 years until it was rediscovered and published in 1940.

Col. Stapleton Crutchfield (1835-1865) served as Jackson's chief of artillery. Jackson had known him as a student at V.M.I., from which Crutchfield graduated in 1855. He then served as a faculty member with Jackson for six years, until the war broke out. In 1861 Crutchfield signed on as major in the 9th Virginia, soon transfering with the same rank to the 58th Virginia, where he rose to lieutenant colonel. In May 1862 he was elected colonel of the 16th Virginia, but declined the position in order to become Jackson's chief of artillery with the rank of colonel. Jackson enjoyed Crutchfield's companionship so much that Stonewall overlooked his friend's fondness for sleeping late.

Crutchfield was wounded at Chancellorsville on 2 May 1863 and left the battlefield in the same ambulance as Jackson, who had been mortally wounded by his own men. Crutchfield subsequently lost a leg to amputation. In May 1864, after a year of convalescence, he took on a job inspecting seacoast batteries. In January 1865 he became commander of an artillery brigade in G.W.C. Lee's division of the Richmond defenses. Crutchfield fell in action during one of the war's last engagements, the battle of Sayler's Creek, on 7 April 1865.

Capt. James K. Boswell, Jackson's chief of engineers, was with Stonewall on the evening of 2 May 1863 when Jackson and some of his mounted staff were returning to their own lines after scouting enemy positions in the twilight. A North Carolina regiment mistook the group for Union cavalry and let loose a volley—Boswell was killed instantly and Jackson was wounded mortally.

CHAPTER III

Lull

March–April 1862

Plans and Reorganization: Union

*T*he repercussions of Kernstown were felt all the way to Washington and had lasting effect on the future course of the War.

McClellan decided that the pesky Jackson had to be dealt with sternly so that he would pose no more problems. On 1 April he told Banks that the Valley theatre would now take on a more important role: "The change in affairs in the valley of the Shenandoah has rendered a corresponding departure—temporary at least—from the plan we some days since agreed on.... The most important thing at present is to throw Jackson back, and then to assume such a position as to enable you to prevent his return. As soon as the railway communications are reestablished, it will be probably important and advisable to move on Staunton, but this would require secure communications and a force of from 25,000 to 30,000 for active operations. It should also be nearly coincident with my own move on Richmond; at all events, not so long before it as to enable the rebels to concentrate on you and then return on me."

What McClellan was now contemplating amounted to a determined effort to drive Jackson from the Valley. On paper, Banks' corps of over 20,000 men in two divisions seemed to be more than enough for this mission—provided that Jackson was

Secretary of War Edwin M. Stanton. The feud between McClellan and Stanton hampered the Union effort in the Valley.

not futher reinforced. This prospect appears not to have been seriously considered by McClellan, perhaps because he did not wish to consider its consequences. In fact, McClellan's plan to move his entire army by sea and approach Richmond from the east actually invited the Confederates to reinforce Jackson or even make a stab at Washington. The latter is exactly what Lincoln and Secretary of War Edwin M. Stanton feared.

Lincoln and Stanton had given McClellan permission to move his army to Fortress Monroe provided that Washington was adequately defended. After McClellan left Washington, Stanton was disturbed to learn that his general had left behind nowhere near the 55,000 men he was supposed to leave. McClellan, quite understandably, had taken his best units with him and left behind regiments that were misfits, green, or poorly equipped. He had also stripped Washington's defenses of almost every available cannoneer, field piece, and horse. To make matters worse, McClellan included Banks' command among the 73,456 men he claimed had been left behind to cover the capital. Banks' men at Winchester were actually in no position to directly aid the defense of Washington. Once Banks began his drive on Staunton, as projected by McClellan, he would be totally out of touch with both Washington and McClellan's army at Fortress Monroe.

Major General George B. McClellan (right) wanted Major General Irvin McDowell (left) to bring his large corps south from Fredericksburg to help him capture Richmond. Jackson's successes in the Valley Campaign prevented McDowell from doing so.

Federal troops take possession of Strasburg, Va., in the wake of Jackson's retreat after Kernstown, one of the few defeats in Jackson's military career.

This situation, of course, was far from pleasing to Lincoln and Stanton. It produced two immediate reactions that would have a profound effect on Jackson in the Valley. Firstly, Lincoln ordered McClellan to detach Maj. Gen. Irvin McDowell's *I Corps* to Manassas to better protect the direct route from Richmond to Washington. McClellan was sorely disturbed to be deprived of McDowell's 30,000-men, but he had set himself up for the aggravation by deliberately undermanning the garrison of Washington.

Lincoln's second reaction was even more far reaching—he reduced McClellan's command from all of Virginia to only the *Army of the Potomac* and those troops directly involved in the drive on Richmond. McDowell was given an autonomous command east of the Blue Ridge with instructions to advance

Brig. Gen. Louis Blenker's German division formed the nucleus of the ill-fated federal XI Corps. Gen. Blenker stands just to the left of center with his hand on his belt.

from Manassas to Fredericksburg, and Banks received a similarly independent command in the Valley, with instructions to take care of Jackson. Lincoln's plan had the advantage of clearly defining objectives and spheres of activity for the three major armies in Virginia. But any advantages brought by this new plan were more than negated by the fact that the movements of Banks, McDowell, and McClellan were to be coordinated by Lincoln himself, and not by an experienced or qualified general. Lincoln's lack of expertise in this area would become painfully clear during the coming campaign.

The command structure in Virginia had been further clouded on 11 March when Lincoln created yet another department in Virginia, the *Mountain Department* (formerly the *Department of Western Virginia*). This department was to be commanded by Maj. Gen. John C. Frémont, another of the war's "also rans" who were attracted to such minor departments. Frémont had the brainstorm of marching from western Virginia to seize Knoxville, Tennessee, a center of pro-Unionist sentiment that President Lincoln dearly longed to recover. The fact that Knoxville was 300 miles from Frémont's base did not dissuade

Lincoln from approving the expedition; the President even directed McClellan to reinforce Frémont with a fresh division, Brig. Gen. Louis Blenker's, of which more will be heard shortly. Blenker was directed to march his 10,000 men to join Frémont via Strasburg, but Banks was authorized to detain Blenker if he were needed in order to deal with Jackson.

Plans and Reorganization: Confederate

Jackson did not know of, nor did he have time to consider, these developments as he patched his battered army together after Kernstown. Following the battle, his men had retreated to the Valley Turnpike and thence to Newtown, about six miles to the south of the battlefield. Jackson himself spent the night of 23-24 March on a bed of fence rails after enjoying a brief supper that broke his day-long fast. The next morning his weary army limped towards Mount Jackson, where the brief campaign had started. Over the next week he regrouped his command and then took up a defensive posture south of the Shenandoah's North Fork, at a plateau called Rude's Hill. For the next two weeks, no contact occurred with the enemy beyond some skirmishing by Ashby's cavalry near Edinburg. The weather was cold and rainy, and neither side was immediately disposed towards offensive operations.

Meanwhile, Jackson had a few internal problems to deal with. First was the matter of his anger at Richard Garnett for withdrawing without orders at Kernstown. On 1 April, just over a week after the battle, Jackson placed Garnett under arrest and relieved him of duty. As formally drawn up, the charges against him included seven specifications concerning his alleged misconduct at Kernstown. The key specification claimed that "Garnett gave the order to fall back when he should have encouraged his command to hold its position." The crux of the charge was actually that Garnett should have consulted Jackson beforehand about withdrawing; the men of the Stonewall Brigade were in fact well aware that Garnett had saved the unit from destruction by his withdrawal order. After Garnett was arrested, his men were so annoyed with Jackson that for quite some time they kept a stony silence whenever Stonewall passed

Confederate William B. Taliaferro. Seen as a "political"general despite Mexican War experience, he served effectively throughout the Valley campaign despite many differences with Jackson.

by. For the same reason, the men of the Stonewall Brigade took a long time to accept Brig. Gen. Charles Winder, who on 2 April took over the brigade as Garnett's replacement.

Jackson's other two brigades also underwent command changes at this time. Colonel Burks, the uninspired commander of the army's 2nd Brigade, requested sick leave, and Jackson seized upon the opportunity to ask Richmond for a replacement. When none was forthcoming, he assigned the brigade temporarily to its senior regimental commander, Colonel John Campbell of the 48th Virginia. It is interesting to note that Richmond would not send a replacement for Burks, but Joe Johnston did order William Taliaferro to return to Jackson's command. Taliaferro had been transferred from Jackson's army in the hubbub over Romney (See Chapter 1). Now, freshly promoted to brigadier general through his political connections, Taliaferro was returning to action under Jackson. By Johnston's orders, Taliaferro was to be given command of Jackson's 3rd Brigade, which Col. Samuel V. Fulkerson had been handling quite well. Fulkerson was then returned to the command of his 37th Virginia regiment.

Another set of problems Jackson faced at this juncture was centered on recruiting his army back to strength. He worked hard for several weeks to bring up militia units, train them, and then convert them into regular army units. In this endeavor he was aided by a Confederate law that required military service of all able-bodied men between the ages of 18 and 35. Several militia units, however, resisted conversion to regular Confederate service. Among these was the Rockingham militia, which was not brought into obedience until Jackson sent a combined force of infantry, cavalry and artillery under Lieutenant Col. J.R. Jones of the 33rd Virginia to subdue them. During this same period Jackson was busy reorganizing the one-year units whose members now lacked the enthusiasm they had shown when they originally enlisted in April of 1861 in the first wave of patriotic fervor that followed the capture of Fort Sumter.

As Jackson reorganized his army, he developed his plans for the coming campaign. He wrote his superiors that in his present situation he could do no more than remain on the defensive. What he preferred to do was to take the offensive against Banks, but to do this he needed heavy reinforcements. Jackson's request did not fall on sympathetic ears in Richmond. Davis and Johnston were well aware that McClellan had gathered an enormous army to attack Richmond, and every available Confederate soldier would be needed to defend the capital. Once it became clear that McClellan's main thrust would come from the area of Fortress Monroe, Johnston began shifting his army to the peninsula between the James and York Rivers. Maj. Gen. Richard "Dick" Ewell's division was left to guard the northern approaches to Richmond, with instructions to coordinate his movements with Jackson. Jackson was directed to oppose Banks as best he could, with the primary purpose of defending Staunton and the Virginia Central Railroad, which was one of Richmond's key supply lines. There would be no reinforcements for Jackson, and he would have to stand on his own as best he could. For the moment Jackson would have to limit his movements to reacting to those of his opponent. Thus, his preparations made, he awaited Banks' next move. It did not take Banks long to begin his spring campaign.

The Preliminaries

On 16 April Banks sent Shields' division marching south from Woodstock. Shields was at first opposed solely by Ashby's cavalry, which had been sparring with its blue-clad counterparts ever since Kernstown. This time it was the Yankees who got the upper hand. Near Columbia Furnace, Shields' advance surprised and captured a company of 50 men with all their gear. It seems that the company commander, a Captain Harper, had neglected to post pickets that night, and so fully deserved the disaster that befell him.

Jackson had planned to make a defensive stand at Rude's Hill, but his strategy was confounded by another lapse on the part of Ashby's cavalry. The key to the Rude's Hill position was the fact that the northern approaches were entirely fronted by several bends of the North Fork of the Shenandoah River. To aid his own mobility, Jackson had left intact the key bridge over the river; Ashby's cavalry had been assigned the task of burning the bridge when the army fell back to its final defensive line on Rude's Hill.

Early on the morning of 17 April the Federals put heavy pressure on Ashby's rear guard. Most of the Confederate cavalry thundered across the Shenandoah bridge, leaving behind a 12-man detachment under Captain John Winfield with orders to burn the bridge. Winfield's men lighted their kindling as ordered, and then fired two volleys into the Federals who were attacking them. Yet the Federals did not stop. A squadron of their cavalry ran right across the burning bridge and through Winfield's command. They then jumped on Ashby's main force and came within a hair of bagging Ashby himself. Ashby and his men made a mad dash for Jackson's main line on Rude's Hill, and barely got there ahead of their blue-clad pursuers. Meanwhile, another force of Yankees put out the fire on the bridge, clearing the way for Shields' entire division to cross.

Jackson, needless to say, was quite disheartened to see Ashby's cavalry routed and the invaluable Shenandoah bridge fall intact to the enemy. Now that the enemy had crossed the river safely, he was unable to hold Rude's Hill. For this reason, Jackson wasted no time ordering a withdrawal to the south. He also realized that it was time to call on Ewell for help. Joe Johnston had authorized him to call on Ewell if he were pressed too hard and could no longer hold the Valley. At 1450 on 17 April Jackson sent an order to Ewell to meet him at Swift Run Gap in the Blue Ridge Mountains.

Upon retreating from Rude's Hill, Jackson withdrew to Harrisonburg. But from Harrisonburg, he did not continue south to Staunton as Banks expected. Instead, he marched his troops east around the southern end of the Massanutten Mountains and bivouacked at Conrad's Store, 20 miles east of Harrisonburg. There he awaited Ewell's arrival at nearby Swift Run Gap. Jackson's plan was to take advantage of the Shenandoah's geography to make one of two possible movements-to attack the right flank of any Union force moving on Staunton, or to rush up the Luray Valley and get into the Union rear through the New Market Gap or at Front Royal, where the Massanutten Mountains abruptly ended.

Jackson waited ten days for Ewell's force to arrive. In this period his own strength increased to about 6000 through further enlistments. In spite of Ewell's pending approach, Jackson still wanted more men from Richmond to reinforce his army so that he could take the offensive against Banks. On 28 April Gen. R.E. Lee wrote Jackson that he could spare no reinforcements for the Valley from Fredericksburg or Richmond. However, Jackson might be able to get support from Brig. Gen. Edward "Allegheny" Johnson's command of 3000 men that was then posted in the mountains west of Staunton. Johnson was facing two brigades of Frémont's Union army, a force of 6000 led by Brig. Gen. Robert Schenck and Robert Milroy.

The availability of Johnson's command caused Jackson to alter his strategic plans. He now decided to concentrate his own, Ewell's, and Johnson's commands (about 17,000 men) against Banks' corps of 19,000 at Harrisonburg. However, Frémont's corps of 15,000 was a concern in the western mountains. If Frémont joined Banks at Staunton, Jackson would have no chance of recovering the Valley. To prevent this, Jackson had to act quickly. The more vulnerable of the two opponents was Frémont, whose brigades were strung out in the western mountains. Most vulnerable of all were Brig. Gen. Robert C. Schenck and Brig. Gen. Robert H. Milroy, commanding Frémont's advance units. A quick Confederate strike might be able to destroy these two brigades before they could be reinforced by the rest of Frémont's army, which was then near Moorefield and Romney.

Before beginning the next stage of the Valley campaign, Jackson made several key additions to his staff. Henry Kyd Douglas, a lieutenant in the 2nd Virginia, was made an aide, and Lt. Col. Stapleton Crutchfield accepted the important post of Chief of Artillery. A third newcomer was the Rev. Robert L. Dabney, the new Assistant Adjutant General (chief of staff). These additions to the likes of master mapmaker Jedediah Hotchkiss and chief surgeon Hunter McGuire made Jackson's staff one of the best assembled during the war by any general. Stonewall would certainly need the skills of every one of his staff members in the coming hectic weeks, for he was now ready to begin his Valley campaign in earnest.

The German Division

Perhaps the most unlucky unit in the *Army of the Potomac* was Brig. Gen. Louis Blenker's division. It was an all-foreign unit whose regiments included the *Garibaldi Guard*, *(39th New York)*, *DeKalb Regiment (41st New York)*, *Schwarze Jaegers (54th New York)*, and *Polish Legion (58th New York)*. Though there were Italians, Poles, Hungarians and many other foreigners in the division, most of its men were of German background, and it was informally called "The German Division." The division's commanders included Hungarian-born Brig. Gen. Julius Stahel, German-born Brig. Gen. Adolph von Steinwehr, and colonels such as Vladimir Krzyzanowski and Leopold von Gilsa. The *Army of the Potomac* had ambiguous feelings about the foreigners in Blenker's division. Since so many of Blenker's men had previous military experience in Europe, their skills were highly valued. However, the racism encouraged by the strange accents and uniforms of many of Blenker's men caused Blenker's command to be viewed with suspicion and distrust. Driven by these considerations, in the spring of 1862 the War Department decided to detach the division from McClellan's *II Corps* and send it as reinforcement to Maj. Gen. John C. Frémont in the Mountain Department of western Virginia, for Frémont enjoyed great favor among German-Americans, and was thought to be the general best qualified to deal with Blenker's men. Since Frémont was crying for reinforcements, Blenker's division seemed the best choice to send.

Blenker was also directed to cooperate with Banks against Jackson while he traveled west, if the occasion demanded.

Blenker's trek west from Warrenton Junction was one of the unchronicled fiascoes of the war. Blenker's problems began only two days after his departure. On 7 April an unusual spring snowstorm caught the division at Salem. Besides making the roads virtually impassable, the storm caused immeasurable discomfort to the men, who had no foul weather gear and no tents, for they had left their camp tents near Arlington and had never been issued shelter tents. As a result, the men had to sleep in the open during the whole march under unstable spring skies. The division also had left behind most of its medical supplies, and had very few ambulances for the sick. On 8 April the march continued through a storm that produced both rain and snow. Progress slowed greatly, and soon the men had consumed all the provisions they had brought with them. They then realized that nobody had made arrangements to resupply them while they were "in transit" between departments. Consequently, they had no choice but to resort to foraging and pillaging to survive. Even this was difficult because parts of the march passed through places where they could not find "forage enough for a mule." Another problem was the lack of accurate maps. Blenker kept getting lost, and ended up spending nearly three weeks traveling only about fifty miles to Harpers Ferry. It took him an additional three weeks to reach Frémont at Moorefield. General Banks, the Union commander in the lower Shenandoah Valley, was supposed to look out for Blenker and forward him to Frémont. However, Banks did little more than report Blenker's wanderings to Frémont.

When Blenker failed to reach Harpers Ferry promptly, both Frémont and the War Department began to worry. Finally, on 12 April the War Department took the unusual step of appointing Brig. Gen. William S. Rosecrans to find Blenker and take him and his men to Frémont. Rosecrans managed to locate the Germans near Berry's Ferry on the Shenandoah. Here, the *75th Pennsylvania* had just met an unfortunate accident. On April 15, a boat carrying *Companies I* and *K* of the regiment had sunk, drowning 51 men and two officers.

When Rosecrans found Blenker's men, he was appalled at their condition and began gently shepherding them towards Winchester. In a letter to Frémont dated 19 April 1862, Rosecrans reported, "We are bivouacked five miles out of Winchester, after thirty-eight days without tents or shelter. Troops wanting shoes, provisions and forage. Horses much jaded and nearly starved." Other missives requested 36 ambulances, and 42 horses to move batteries. Blenker's men were, in fact, in such

bad shape that they were unable to function at anything near full capacity during the upcoming campaign. The army's medical director and other officers noted their worn-out condition and the straggling it caused.

When Blenker's men finally did get into battle, at Cross Keys on 8 June, they did not acquit themselves at all well. In fact, the Germans did not enjoy much success in any battle. In late June of 1862 Blenker's division became the nucleus of the *I Corps* in John Pope's *Army of Virginia*. As such, it fought in the defeat at Second Bull Run. Redesignated the *XI Corps* of the *Army of the Potomac*, the Germans missed the battles of Antietam and Fredericksburg. They were then so thoroughly routed at Chancellorsville and the first day of Gettysburg that the corps was broken up on 5 August 1863. Some of the corps' regiments were sent west to Tennessee, but most were sent to the swamps of South Carolina to assist in the siege of Charleston. The experiment of having a Union division, and then corps, composed almost entirely of foreign-born troops had been a failure because of biases, poor generalship, and bad luck—but not because of lack of devotion and heroism among the foreign-born soldiers.

Stonewall's Faith

It would seem strange that so religious a man as Jackson was.a general by occupation—how could he justify leading men to death and destruction if he were such a devout Christian? He was driven by motives different from those of Robert E. Lee, a devout Christian, who deplored war but fought because he thought it was his duty to defend himself and his home. It seems clear that Jackson was driven by an overwhelming sense of ambition to succeed and gain fame by force of arms. This explains why he so often pushed himself and his men beyond what was reasonable or even possible. We are not now in a position to judge what came first in Jackson's eyes, glory or God; most likely the two were one and the same.

Stonewall's feelings about glory and God are clearly shown in a letter to his wife on 22 July 1861, the day after First Bull Run: "My Precious Pet—Yesterday we fought a great battle and gained a great victory, for which all the glory is due to God alone. Although under a heavy fire for several continuous hours, I received only one wound, the breaking of the longest finger of my left hand; but the doctor says the finger can be saved. It was broken about midway between the hand and knuckle, the ball passing on the side next the forefinger. Had it struck the centre, I should have lost the finger. My horse was wounded, but not killed. Your coat got an ugly wound near the hip, but my servant, who is very handy, has so far repaired it that it doesn't show very much. My preservation was entirely due, as was the glorious victory, to our God, to whom be all the honor, praise, and glory. The battle was the hardest that I have ever been in, but not near so hot in its fire. I commanded in the centre more particularly, though one of my regiments extended to the right for some distance. There were other commands on my right and left. Whilst great credit is due to other parts of our gallant army, God made my brigade more instrumental than any other in repulsing the main attack. This is for your information only—say nothing about it. Let others speak praise, not myself."

Jackson was not deeply devoted to the Church until the prime of his life. In his early years he attended no particular church. His mother was reportedly a member of the Methodist faith, but young Thomas was affiliated with no specific church during his troubled early years. His first lengthy exposure to organized religion probably came at West Point, where he became accustomed to the Academy's Episcopal services. Nevertheless, he did not show deep interest in the Church until his stay in Mexico City in 1847–1848. There he experimented with several sects until he was reintroduced to Episcopalianism by Col. Francis Taylor, the commander of the 1st Artillery. His dedication then became so deep that he was baptized under Colonel Taylor's sponsorship on 29 April 1849 at Fort Hamilton, New York, where he was doing garrison duty.

On settling in Lexington, Jackson investigated the local churches and found himself attracted to the Presbyterian church, the largest and most influential in town. He particularly appreciated the church's simple style and the preaching of its devout minister, Dr. William S. White. Jackson made a public profession of his faith at the Lexington Presbyterian church on 21 November 1851. He entered the church with zeal, seeing himself as a warrior "clad in ministerial armor, fighting under the banner of Jesus." As evidence of his faith, he began a Sunday school for Negroes, to which he continued to contribute until his death.

As a devout Presbyterian, Jackson tried to avoid all military activities, especially fighting, on Sundays. Yet war allows no reprieves, and at times he had no choice but to make war contrary to his conscience. Particularly regretful to him were the Sunday battles at Kernstown (23 March 1862), Winchester (25 May 1862), and Port Republic (8 June 1862). To make amends for the Sunday battle at Winchester, he ordered his troops to have a day of rest and thanksgiving, with church services, the following Monday. When reprimanded by his wife for fighting at Kernstown on a Sunday, he replied, "You appear much concerned at my attacking on Sunday. I was greatly concerned, too; but I felt it my duty to do it, in consideration of the ruinous effects that might result from postponing the battle until the morning. So far as I can see, my course was a wise one; the best that I could do under the circumstances, though very distasteful to my feelings; and I hope and pray to our Heavenly Father that I may never again be circumstanced as on that day. I believed that so far as our troops were concerned, necessity and mercy both called for battle. I do hope the war will soon be over, and that I shall never again have to take the field. Arms is a profession that, if its principles are adhered to for success, requires an officer to do what he fears may be wrong, and yet, according to military experience, must be done, if success is to be attained. And this fact of its being necessary to success, and being accompanied with success, and that a departure from it is accompanied with disaster, suggests that it must be right. Had I fought the battle on Monday instead of Sunday, I fear our cause would have suffered; whereas, as things turned out, I consider our cause gained much from the engagement."

Thus, Jackson was not above fighting on a Sunday if it were necessary or to his military advantage. Occasionally, though, he did put off necessary military activity that was called for on a Sunday. One notable case was on 22 June 1862, when he was pushing his troops hard to reach Richmond in time to attack the Yankees before they were aware of his arrival. Though time was of the essence in this movement, he kept his troops in camp all day. His reasons were those expressed to Reverend Dabney on another similar occasion: "The Sabbath is written in the constitution of man and horses as really as in the Bible: I can march my men farther in a week, marching six days and resting the seventh, and get through with my men and horses in better condition than if I marched them all seven days."

Jackson's Personal Habits

Stonewall Jackson's personal habits were such that he was known as an eccentric even back in his days as a Professor at V.M.l. He usually wore an old army jacket, and was not impressive to behold. One soldier described him as "an ungraceful horseman, mounted on a sorry chestnut with a shambling gait, his huge feet with outturned toes thrust into his stirrups, and such parts of his countenance as the low visor of his stocking cap failed to conceal wearing a wooden look."

Jackson would often sit still for hours or stare blankly at his troops as they marched by. His men thought this strange, but they came to accept his way, believing that he was meditating or planning future battles. He was noted for being reticent, except with his closest staff members, with whom he only occasionally carried on friendly conversations; it was quite an aberration the night in the Romney campaign that he became garrulous after drinking too much alcoholic "anti-freeze."

Jackson's most eccentric trait was perhaps his habit of sucking lemons. He seems to have done this because it helped (or, he thought it helped) a nervous stomach. Whatever the reason, he was rarely without one, and his men felt he would be very uncomfortable without any. Where he got them, nobody knew.

Jackson's strange personal behavior was perhaps most succinctly described by Dick Taylor, who wrote, "If silence be golden, he was a bonanza. He sucked lemons, ate hard tack, and drank water, and praying and fasting appeared to be his idea of the 'whole duty of man.'"

A fuller character sketch was penned by Jackson's aide, Henry Kyd Douglas. "In face and figure Jackson was not striking. Above the average height, with a frame angular, muscular and fleshless, he was, in all his movements from riding a horse to handling a pen, the most awkward man in the army. His expression was thoughtful, and, as a result I fancy of his long ill health, was generally clouded with an air of fatigue. His eye was small, blue, and in repose as gentle as a young girl's. With high, broad forehead, small sharp nose, thin pallid lips generally held shut, deep-set eyes, dark rusty beard, he was certainly not a handsome man. His face in tent or parlor, softened by his sweet smile, was as different from itself on the battlefield as a little lake in summer noon differs from the same lake when frozen. . . . The enemy believed he never slept. In fact he slept a great deal. Give him five minutes to rest, he could sleep three of them. Whenever he had nothing else to do he went to sleep, especially in church. He could sleep in any position, in a chair, under fire, or on horseback.... He was quiet, not morose. He often smiled, rarely laughed. He never told a joke but rather liked to hear one, now and then, He did not live apart from his personal staff, although they were nearly all young; he liked to have them about, especially at table. He encouraged the liveliness of their conversation, although he took little part in it. His own words seemed to embarrass him, unless he could follow his language by action. As he never told his plans, he never discussed them. He didn't offer advice to his superiors, or ask it of his subordinates."

Jackson's Horses

During the war Stonewall Jackson owned three horses of which he was especially fond. One, named Boy, was a carriage horse he bought for his wife shortly before the war. In July of 1861 he bought a small, rather rotund horse from those he captured aboard a Federal train on the Baltimore and Ohio Railroad. The horse was named Fancy, which was quite a misnomer because of its features and great size. The horse nevertheless became quite a pet, and had the strange habit of lying down like a dog when ordered to stop and rest. Jackson's favorite horse was the famous Little Sorrel, which he preferred because his gait was "as easy as the rocking of a cradle." Jackson rode him in nearly every battle, though he owned several larger steeds. Sorrel was lost for a while after Stonewall was mortally wounded at Chancellorsville, but was found and returned to Mrs. Jackson. The horse outlived its master by 23 years, dying in 1886 at an age of over 30 years.

CHAPTER IV

The McDowell Operation

30 April–20 May 1862

*T*he new campaign began on 30 April when Jackson started his men marching southeast from Conrad's Store towards Port Republic. His men were certain that they were headed for a confrontation with Banks, but their hopes were dashed when they reached Port Republic and then turned southeast, away from Banks and out of the Valley. The men now became as dejected as they had been happy. The roads were a sea of mud, and great effort had to be made just to make them passable for infantry, let alone for artillery and wagons. Finally the exhausted command dragged into Mechum's Station on the Virginia Central Railroad. The troops then boarded trains, convinced that they were headed for Richmond, leaving their beloved Valley undefended before Banks' minions.

Imagine the pleasure of Jackson's men when they realized the trains they boarded at Mechum's Station were heading west, not east. On 4 May Jackson's troops began entering Staunton, which miraculously had not yet been occupied by the Federals. In fact, instead of pressing on to Staunton, Banks was actually preparing to move in the other direction. Jackson's movements had convinced Banks that the Confederates were on their way to Richmond. Since Jackson's supposed withdrawal accomplished Banks' mission in the Valley, Banks was preparing to return up the Valley and march east to cover Washington and perhaps even join McClellan's army, the same movement he had been attempting at the time of Kernstown.

When Jackson heard of Banks' withdrawal to the north, he realized that the time was ripe to strike at Frémont's advance brigade under Milroy. On the 6th he sent Allegheny Johnson's command (which had previously joined Jackson at Staunton) to establish and keep contact with Milroy. Jackson followed Johnson on the 7th, and was soon only a half day's march behind Johnson's column.

Meanwhile, the wary Milroy realized that something was up. He knew that at least part of Jackson's command had joined Johnson, so he withdrew to a defensive position along the Bull Pasture River, just east of McDowell. There he awaited the arrival of Schenck's brigade, which was on its way to join him from Franklin. By forced marches, Schenck reached Milroy at noon on the 9th.

These two brigades of no more 6000 men, however, would be no match for the 10,000 under Johnson and Jackson. Stonewall was on the march before 0500 on 8 May, and his troops began reaching Johnson's command in midafternoon. Jackson, who arrived ahead of his vanguard, found Johnson formed on a plateau called Sitlington's Hill that was actually a branch of Bull Pasture Mountain. Jackson noted that the Union position behind Bull Pasture River was so strong that he would not be able to venture an attack until his whole force was up, which would not happen for at least a couple hours. While Jackson awaited the balance of his army, the Union commander decided to try the unexpected.

McDowell, 8 May 1862

General Milroy was aware of Johnson's arrival opposite McDowell and knew that the Confederate strength would grow as the afternoon progressed. Around 1600 Milroy decided to make a bold attack on Johnson's position before the Confederates received any more reinforcements. Following a brief and effective artillery barrage, the Federals crossed the Bull Pasture River and began engaging Johnson's skirmishers. Because of dense woods and the lay of the ground, Milroy's men were able

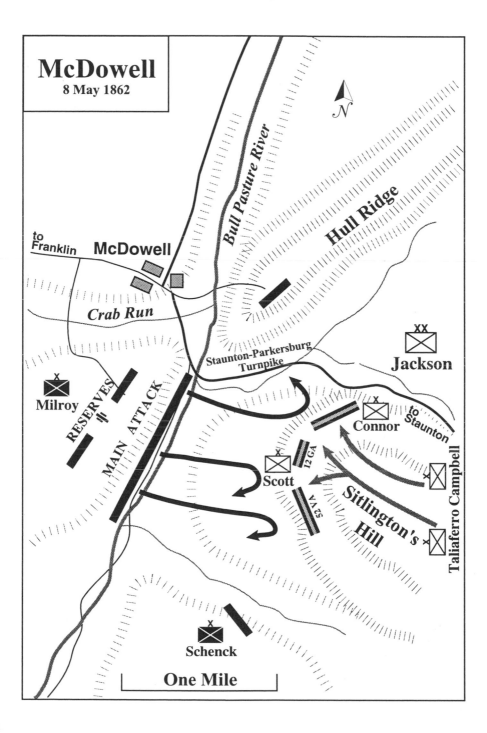

McDowell
8 May 1862

Bull Pasture River

Hull Ridge

to Franklin

McDowell

Crab Run

N

Staunton-Parkersburg Turnpike

Jackson

Milroy

RESERVES

MAIN ATTACK

Connor

to Staunton

12 GA

Scott

52 VA

Sitlington's Hill

Taliaferro Campbell

Schenck

One Mile

Brig. Gen. Edward "Allegh-eny" Johnson held field command at the battle of McDowell until he was wounded in the foot. He later commanded Jackson's old division from Gettysburg through Spotsylvania.

to approach quite close to Johnson's lines before becoming heavily engaged.

As the battle developed, the Confederates began to find themselves hard pressed. The contours of Sitlington's Hill forced Johnson to deploy in a long crescent line with his flanks turned back from the enemy. Johnson had posted his best regiment, the 12th Georgia, in the center; he had the 52nd and 58th Virginia on the left, the 44th Virginia on the right, and 25th and 31st Virginia in reserve. After being initially repulsed, Milroy began pressing Johnson's right. Johnson responded by committing his reserves to that sector. Soon, however, Union pressure was renewed, as Schenck's fresh troops were committed to the fight. After an hour of combat, some of Johnson's men began to run out of ammunition and the situation looked grim indeed for the Confederates. The center of the Rebel line was in particular trouble because it lay in the open and lacked cover. Here the proud 12th Georgia stood and took its casualties rather than withdraw in dishonor. On other parts of the line, the gray-clad infantrymen were easy targets for the enemy, being silhouetted against the late afternoon sky.

It was at this juncture that Jackson's own troops began reaching the field. Taliaferro's brigade was the first, and his three regiments were immediately thrown into the fray. The

A portrait of Jackson taken during the Mexican war. He served with distinction in the artillery during almost every battle from Vera Cruz to the capture of Mexico City.

23rd and 37th Virginia were sent to the center to assist the 12th Georgia, and succeeded in stabilizing the line there. Taliaferro's third regiment, the 10th Virginia, and Campbell's brigade were sent to the right. Just as the Confederates were taking control of the battle, General Johnson was badly wounded in the ankle. Up until then Jackson had been staying in the background, letting his subordinate run the battle. Now that Johnson was wounded, Stonewall took charge and mopped up the victory. As darkness began to fall, Milroy and Schenck realized that their attack had failed and withdrew across the river at about 2100. They then burned Milroy's camp and retreated north towards Franklin and the rest of Frémont's army.

McDowell was clearly a Confederate victory, even though Jackson's losses far outnumbered those of the Yankees. When the tallies had been made, Jackson casualties were found to be 75 killed and 428 wounded out of 6000 total engaged; 175 of these casualties came from the 12th Georgia alone. Milroy and Schenck had only about half that number engaged, and reported only 256 casualties: 28 killed, 225 wounded, and three missing or captured. Clearly the Yankees, though defeated, had out-fought the Confederates at McDowell. The Southerners had the clear advantage of a good defensive position and superior strength, yet they had lost over 65 percent more casualties than their attackers. Milroy's bold attack had almost worked, and might well have succeeded if the troops in Jackson's column had not been so prompt in reinforcing Johnson's hard pressed command.

Jackson's despatch to Richmond announcing his victory at McDowell was as succinct as Caesar's *"Veni, vidi, vici"*:

> Valley District,
> May 9, 1862
> To Gen. S. Cooper:
> God blessed our arms with victory at McDowell yesterday.
> —T.J. Jackson, Major-General

March and Countermarch, 9-18 May

After resting his army on 9 May, Jackson began to pursue Schenck and Milroy as they retreated north. His immediate goal was not to fight them again, though he certainly would not have refused a battle if one were offered; instead, Jackson simply wanted to drive Frémont's forces as far as possible into the mountains so that they could not immediately march to join Banks. To assure that the two enemy armies would not be able to link up, Stonewall sent his most reliable staff member, Jed Hotchkiss, to gather up some trustworthy cavalry to block the mountain passes between Harrisonburg on the east and McDowell and Franklin on the west. Hotchkiss carried out his orders as Jackson commanded. He burned every bridge he crossed, cut down trees to block the passes at North River Gap, Dry River Gap, and Brocks' Gap, and for good measure rolled large boulders across the roads that passed through the gaps. To keep Jackson informed of his progress, Hotchkiss despatched a courier every hour, as Stonewall had requested.

Meanwhile Jackson was having difficulty keeping contact with Schenck's and Milroy's force. As they retreated, the Yankees started forest fires that obscured their route with dense smoke. Reverend Robert L. Dabney of Jackson's staff observed, "Soon the sky was overcast with volumes of smoke which almost hid the scene, and wrapped every distant object in a veil impenetrable to the eyes and the telescopes of the officers alike. Through this sultry fog the pursuing army felt its way very cautiously along, cannonaded by the enemy from every advantageous position, while it was protected from ambuscades only by detachments of skirmishers who scoured the burning woods on each side of the highway. As fast as these could scramble over the precipitous hills and the blazing thickets, the great column crept along the main road like a lazy serpent, the general often far in advance of its head, in his eagerness to overtake the foe. He declared that this smoke was the most adroit expedient to which a retreating army could resort to embarrass pursuit, and that it entailed upon him all the disadvantages of a night attack."

By such measures, Milroy and Schenck kept well ahead of Jackson, and reached Franklin (30 miles north of McDowell) safely on 11 May. Jackson's army arrived later that day and began skirmishing with the enemy, even though it was the Sabbath. To make up for this "sacrilege," Jackson issued the following order on 12 May:

> Soldiers of the Army of the Valley and Northwest:
> I congratulate you on your recent victory at McDowell. I request you to unite with me this morning in thanksgiving to Almighty God for thus having crowned your arms with success, and in praying that he will continue to lead you on from victory to victory until our independence shall be established, and make us that people whose God is the Lord. The chaplains will hold Divine Service at 10 o'clock A.M. this day, in their respective regiments.

Jackson now decided that the purpose of his Allegheny expedition had been achieved—he had defeated Milroy and Schenck, relieved the pressure on Staunton, and driven Frémont's advance brigades all the way back to Franklin, some 50 miles from Staunton. Since Jed Hotchkiss had blocked the passes leading directly from Franklin to the Valley, Frémont would have to march via Moorefield and Strasburg in order to reach Banks. Such a march would be slow and tedious because of the mountainous roads. In effect, Jackson had driven Frémont out of the campaign for a couple of weeks at least.

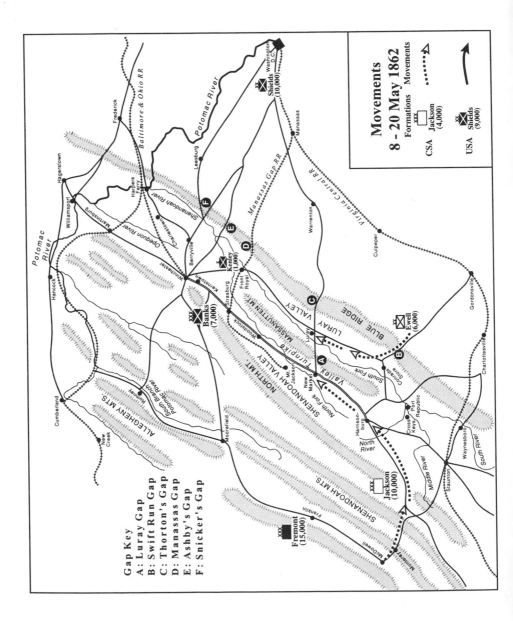

Gap Key
A: Luray Gap
B: Swift Run Gap
C: Thorton's Gap
D: Manassas Gap
E: Ashby's Gap
F: Snicker's Gap

Movements
8 - 20 May 1862

Formations   Movements

CSA   USA

Jackson
(4,000)

Shields
(9,000)

Jackson's next problem was to decide what course of action would now be suitable. Since Frémont had gathered most of his army in support of Milroy and Schenck at Franklin, the Confederates had little prospect of fighting and winning a victory there. Jackson's preference was to return to the Valley, join Ewell, and give Banks a thrashing. However, Stonewall feared that affairs in the valley had gotten out of hand while he was conducting the McDowell operation. Banks had withdrawn in preparation for departing to the east, and R.E. Lee in Richmond was considering sending Ewell alone in pursuit of Banks.

Jackson now headed his men back to the Valley. His army left Franklin on the afternoon of 12 May, and reached McDowell on the 14th. On the 15th he headed for Staunton. Despite the need for swiftness, Jackson kept his men in camp on 16 May to honor a day of fasting and prayer proclaimed by President Jefferson Davis for observation throughout the Confederacy. Stonewall then resumed his march on Saturday 17 May. On the 18th he met with Dick Ewell at Mount Solon, and the two generals set about deciding how best to deal with Banks.

The Northern Shenandoah, 30 April-18 May 1862

While Jackson was in the western mountains, Union Maj. Gen. Nathaniel P. Banks had withdrawn all the way to Strasburg. The first stage of his withdrawal had begun at the beginning of May, as soon as he heard of Ewell's arrival. He was afraid that Jackson and Ewell might join forces to crush him, so he withdrew to New Market. While at New Market, he was ordered to send Shields' division to Fredericksburg to join McDowell's corps, which was preparing to march on Richmond from the north. Banks' command, now reduced from 20,000 to 8,000, was relegated to garrison duty in the lower Shenandoah. Accordingly, Banks withdrew to his supply base at Strasburg, where he posted most of his command; a small force of 1000 men under Col. John R. Kenly was sent to nearby Front Royal to guard the important Shenandoah River bridges there.

Lincoln's decision to strip Banks of Shields' division proved to be a key error in the managing of the campaign. Shields' departure left Banks with scarcely enough men to face Ewell

Major General John C. Frémont was the Republican party's first candidate for president in 1856. He is better remembered as an explorer and politician than for his military accomplishments during the Civil War.

alone; if Jackson and Ewell joined forces, Banks would really be in for trouble. Lincoln and his advisers may have been confused by Jackson's disappearance from Banks' front in early May. When Jackson turned up in the western mountains a few days later, Lincoln assumed that Frémont could handle him and that Jackson by transferring his force there had taken himself out of the Valley theatre for quite a time.

Lincoln's assumptions proved mistaken, for he greatly underestimated Jackson's ability to disengage from Frémont's front and return quickly to the Valley. Lincoln also overestimated Frémont's ability to move quickly and act decisively. Following Jackson's departure from Franklin, Frémont spent a full ten days reorganizing his command before he reentered the campaign. In addition, Blenker's division, which had been loaned to Frémont by McDowell, was so exhausted when it reached the western mountains that it would not be much use for the next month.

While Jackson was fighting Milroy and Schenck, Ewell was left in a dilemma. He had been ordered to cooperate with Jackson, and Jackson had ordered him to remain in Swift Run

General Robert E. Lee was serving as a military adviser to President Jefferson Davis during most of the Valley Campaign. He supported Jackson's plans as much as he could.

Gap in order to keep an eye on Staunton. While Jackson was off in the mountains, however, Ewell kept receiving other suggestions from Lee, who was serving as Jefferson Davis' military advisor in Richmond. On 5 May Lee suggested that Ewell raid the Manassas Gap Railroad; on the 8th he suggested that Ewell move to Gordonsville in order to strike Banks if the latter left the Valley for Fredericksburg. Since Lee had given him no direct order to move, Ewell stayed right where he was for fear of disturbing the irritable Jackson. Ewell was well aware that Jackson had arrested Dick Garnett for insubordination, and he did not want to cross "Old Jack."

When, on 11 May, Ewell heard that Shields was going to leave New Market for Fredericksburg, he longed to attack Shields on the march. However, he was reluctant to do so on his own because of Jackson's orders to remain at Swift Run Gap. When he wrote to Jackson with the news of Shields' departure and asked for instructions, he was amazed to hear Jackson's reply— Stonewall mentioned nothing of Shields, and simply ordered Ewell to pursue Banks closely if the Yankees retreated down the

Valley. This convinced the irascible Ewell that Jackson was indeed crazy. At one point he confided to Col. T.T. Munford of the 2nd Virginia Cavalry, "I could crush Shields before night if I could move from here. This man Jackson is certainly a crazy fool, an idiot. . . . Mark my words, if this old fool keeps things up, and Shields joins McDowell, we will all go up at Richmond." To Col. J.A. Walker of the 13th Virginia he exclaimed, "I tell you, he [Jackson] is as crazy as a March hare!"

Ewell's position became even more unclear on 13 May when Joe Johnston, commander of the army then facing McClellan, reasserted his authority over the Valley District by telling Lee to leave Ewell alone. To Ewell, Johnston wrote: "I have written to Major General Jackson to return to the Valley near you, and, if your united force is strong enough, to attack General Banks. Should the latter cross the Blue Ridge to join General McDowell at Fredericksburg, General Jackson and yourself should move eastward rapidly to join either the army near Fredericksburg or this one. I must be kept informed of your movements and progress, that your instructions may be modified as circumstances change."

Ewell became thoroughly confused on 17 May, when Jackson suggested that the two unite to face Banks. What was Ewell supposed to do? Johnston's orders of the 13th directed him to move east if any Union forces left the Valley, a condition met by Shields' march towards Fredericksburg. Now Jackson wanted him to move north against Banks. Ewell decided the issue by going to meet Jackson face to face at Mount Solon on 18 May.

Strategic Decision, 18–20 May

When Jackson and Ewell conferred at Mount Solon, it seemed obvious that they had to strike at Banks while he was weakened and isolated. This inclination was strengthened by a note Lee sent to Jackson on 16 May: "A successful blow struck at [Banks] would delay, if it does not prevent, his moving. . . . Whatever movement you make against Banks do it speedily and if successful, drive him back toward the Potomac, and create the impression, as far as practicable, that you design threatening that line."

Ewell now finally consented to follow Jackson's orders, since he was in Jackson's department physically and his directions from Johnston were unclear and confusing. It was a bold decision, one that could have ruined Ewell's career if the coming campaign went badly. To help cover his actions, Ewell had Jackson draw up a directive stating, "As you are in the Valley District you constitute part of my command." Jackson, too, was putting his career on the line. If he and Ewell failed to deal with Banks before Shields joined McDowell at Fredericksburg, there was a strong possibility that Richmond might fall to McDowell's overland attack from the north.

The plan of action Jackson and Ewell adopted for the moment was as follows. Jackson, reinforced by Brig. Gen. Richard Taylor's brigade from Ewell's division, would march along the Valley Turnpike, while Ewell marched north through the Luray Valley. Once Banks' position was located, the Confederates would reunite to attack him or bypass him and get into his rear. On the morning of 19 May, Jackson and Ewell began their assigned movements. In order to help disguise their plans, Jackson ordered Ashby to continue fronting Banks' command as he had been doing ever since Jackson left the Valley for McDowell.

The campaign was only two days old when it was halted in mid-course, even as Jackson's army began closing on New Market. On the 20th Jackson received word from Ewell that Joe Johnston had issued an order on 17 May for Ewell to abandon the Valley and join Johnston's army at Richmond. Both Jackson and Ewell were well aware that obedience to this order would mean the end of Jackson's offensive, since Stonewall would be unable to advance alone against Banks. Jackson was so convinced that the proper course was to attack Banks, that he took two steps that verged on insubordination. He sent a telegram to Lee, and directed Ewell to sit still until he received Lee's reply. The telegram read "I am of the opinion that an attempt should be made to defeat Banks, but under instructions just received from General Johnston, I do not feel at liberty to make an attack. Please answer by telegraph at once."

Fortunately for the Confederacy, Lee went to speak with Johnston. He found that Johnston had reevaluated the situation

Front Royal occupied a key position near the confluence of the North and South Forks of the Shenandoah River. Jackson's troops won a victory here on 23 May 1862 prior to the battle of Winchester.

in the Valley. Johnston now realized that it was better for the defense of Richmond if Jackson could defeat Banks and so deflect McDowell's troops from Richmond to the Valley. Late on the 20th he wrote to Jackson, "The object you have to accomplish is the prevention of the junction of Gen. Banks' troops with those of Gen. McDowell." So, after a series of back and forth messages whose sequence is almost too difficult to sort out today, Jackson received permission from his superiors to continue his campaign. Nor can Lee's exact role in the matter now be determined, but there can be little doubt that it was significant. Within hours of receiving Johnston's telegram, Jackson's army resumed its march. And as the troops set out they created a legend.

Jackson's Opponents

The major reason for the Union disasters during the Valley Campaign was that right down the line Federal commanders and command structure were inferior to those of the Confederates. The absence of an overall field commander and interference by Lincoln contributed significantly to lack of coordination among the scattered Union forces. Jackson, on the other hand, had free rein to do what he pleased in order to carry out general directions given by Richmond. The success he enjoyed bears testament as much to his own ability as to the wisdom of the decision to put him in command of the Valley District. As a resident of the Valley, he knew firsthand its quirks of geography and so gained a tremendous homecourt advantage over his opponents.

Unlike Jackson, most of the Union generals in the Valley Campaign were chosen more for their political connections than for their military experience.

Maj. Gen. Nathaniel P. Banks (1816-1894) was a leading Democratic politician before the war, having served several terms as a Massachusetts congressman. He disagreed with Stephen Douglas' Kansas-Nebraska Act, so he switched to the newly formed Republican Party, and as such served as governor of Massachusetts in 1858-1861. Banks' political influence easily won him a commission as major general of volunteers when the war broke out. He had no previous military experience, but had administrative skills from his political career and experience as president of the Illinois Central Railroad.

Banks was soon given command of the *V Corps* of McClellan's *Army of the Potomac,* and was shortly transferred to the lower Shenandoah Valley. There he had the misfortune to face Stonewall Jackson at the height of the Valley Campaign. After his victory at McDowell, Jackson, reinforced by Ewell's division, hurried north to smash Banks' command at Front Royal and Winchester, where Banks lost so many supplies his opponents derisively called him "Commissary Banks." His shattered command played no additional role in the Valley Campaign. Bank's part in the disastrous campaign was investigated, but his name was cleared with Lincoln's support.

After the Valley campaign, Banks' troops became the *II Corps* of Pope's *Army of Virginia.* Banks was in command when his men met Jackson's army at Cedar Mountain on 9 August 1862. He routed the Stonewall Brigade and was carrying the field, only to be driven back by the last minute arrival of A. P. Hill.

These defeats brought Banks a temporary shelving—he was put in command of the defenses of Washington for a month in the fall of 1862. That October he succeeded Benjamin "Beast" Butler as commander of the *Department of the Gulf* at New Orleans, where it was hoped he would need his administrative and political skills more than his military ones. Unfortunately, Banks remained militarily active. During the Vicksburg Campaign he organized the ineffective siege of Port Hudson, Louisiana, which surrendered only when Vicksburg fell. Nevertheless, Banks received the official thanks of Congress "for the skill, courage, and endurance which compelled the surrender of Port Hudson and thus removed the last obstruction to the free navigation of the Mississippi."

Banks' final fling as a field commander came during the infamous Red River Campaign in the spring of 1864. Driven by fuzzy military, economic, and political objectives he may not have fully understood, Banks was defeated by a smaller and more energetic command led by another veteran of Jackson's Valley Campaign, Dick Taylor. Banks resigned from the army after Red River and returned to his first love, politics. He was later elected to six terms as a Massachusetts congressman.

Maj. Gen. James Shields (1806-1879) had a lackluster military career. A native of Ireland, he had been a general in the Mexican War, as well as Democratic governor of Oregon and senator from Oregon and Minnesota. He is said to have challenged Lincoln to a duel once, but later became his friend. Shields was given command of a division in the Valley and led the victorious Union forces at Kernstown, though he had little influence on the course of the battle from his hospital bed in Winchester, having been slightly wounded the night before the battle. Nevertheless, he boasted of the triumph for the rest of his life, claiming that he was the only Union general to defeat Stonewall Jackson in battle.

Shields was also conspicuous for his absence at Port Republic, where he had only two of his four brigades in position to fight Jackson on 9 June. His poor performance there

lost him his command, and he soon resigned from the army in March of 1863.

Maj. Gen. Irvin McDowell (1818-1885), who operated a corps on the periphery of the campaign at Fredericksburg, never fulfilled the promise he appeared to show at the beginning of the war. His prewar experience was earned mostly at a desk and not on the battlefield. After graduating from West Point in 1838 at the age of 20, he became a tactics instructor and administrator at his alma mater. During the Mexican War he was brevetted for service as General Wool's adjutant. Following a brief stint on the Indian frontier, McDowell returned to administrative work at army headquarters in Washington. There his military and political connections won him appointment to the rank of brigadier general when the war broke out. McDowell was given command of the Union field army before Washington, and was put under immense pressure to end the war quickly. After slowly advancing to Centreville, Virginia, he formed a creditable plan for attacking the Confederate positions behind Bull Run. To his misfortune, however, his raw troops were not up to the task, and he had the bad luck of being the attacker in a battle between two green armies in which the advantage definitely fell to the defender.

Strangely, McDowell was not held in particular disgrace for his defeat at First Bull Run. He was demoted from army to division command, but the next spring was promoted to major general in command of *I Corps, Army of the Potomac.* During the Peninsula

Campaign he led the so called *"Army of the Rappahannock"* and as such was on the eastern periphery of Jackson's Valley Campaign. In late June 1862 his corps was re-named the *III Corps* of the *Army of Virginia*. McDowell fought without distinction at Cedar Mountain and Second Bull Run, and was finally sacked by McClellan. He demanded a court of inquiry and had his name cleared of guilt, but was not al-lowed to return to field command. He later served on several military commissions in Washington before being assigned to the Civil War's equivalent of Siberia—he was named commander of the Depart-ment of the Pacific in 1864-1865. McDowell apparently knew no other career, and remained in the army until 1882. He later became park commissioner of the City of San Francisco.

Union Division and Brigade Com-manders. There were strangely only two Union division commanders fighting actively in the campaign (three counting Shields, whose "army" was only a division with at-tached cavalry). Banks had only one division, led by *A. S. Williams* (1810-1878), a solid officer who later led the *XII Corps* briefly at Antietam and Gettysburg. Frémont had seven brigades, only three of which were in division structure. These were German units (later the nucleus of the infamous *XI Corps*) led by *Brig. Gen. Louis Blenker* (1812–1863), a na-tive German. After being defeated by Ewell at Cross Keys, Blenker saw

little additional service and died the next year from injuries received from falling off his horse.

Most Union brigades were led by men who deserved better superiors. Both *Brig. Gen. Erastus B. Tyler* (1822–1891) and *Col. Samuel S. Car-roll* (1832–1893, West Point 1856) spent most of the war as brigade commanders, and both were eventu-ally brevetted major general. Tyler spent most of the war in the Valley, fighting at Kernstown and Mono-cacy in addition to Port Republic. Carroll—who missed a chance to capture Jackson or burn the Port Re-public bridge on the morning of 8 June 1862—fought at Kernstown, Ce-dar Mountain, and Gettysburg. The most famous of Frémont's briga-diers was *Julius Stahel* (1835-1912), a veteran of the 1849 Hungarian Revo-lution who rose to command a divi-sion later in the war. Other foreign brigade commanders with Frémont were *Gustave Cluseret* (1825-1900), a Frenchman who resigned to return home in 1863, and *Henry Bohlen* (1810-1862), a German who was killed in a skirmish two months af-ter Cross Keys.

Frémont's other brigade com-manders were *Robert Milroy* (1816-1890) and *Robert Schenck* (1809-1890). Milroy is best known for his defeat by Ewell at Second Winchester in June 1863; Schenck left the army in 1862 to serve in Con-gress, eventually becoming chair-man of the Committee on Military Affairs.

Maj. Gen. John Charles Frémont

Maj. Gen. John Charles Frémont (1813-1890) is best remembered for his accomplishments as a politician and explorer, not for his military ability. One of the most distinguished men in America before the Civil War broke out, he had joined the army in 1838 as a topographical engineer. His explorations in the Rocky Mountains soon earned him the nickname "The Pathfinder." He happened to be in California in 1846 when hostilities broke out with Mexico. Frémont helped claim the province for the United States and was elected governor, only to be discharged by Gen. Stephen Kearny when the latter arrived with Federal troops and instructions from Washington, D.C. Frémont was then convicted of mutiny and disobedience, but was permitted to resign from the army rather than be dismissed.

Frémont remained in California, becoming one of the state's first U.S. Senators. His political clout was so great that in 1856 he was the first candidate for President put forward by the newly formed Republican Party. Despite his defeat by Democrat James Buchanan, Frémont retained national political influence, particularly among German-Americans. In 1861 these connections won him an appointment as major general in charge of the important Western Department.

Frémont was faced by a whole host of problems, which he helped exacerbate by his own style of command. There were few supplies for his troops, and a strong secessionist element openly flew the Confederate flag. Many objected to the foreign born adventurers who were attracted to his staff, who had strange accents and manners like Hungarian Major Charles Zagonyi. In order to be able to get more work done, Frémont limited civilian access to his headquarters. Local leaders objected to this, particularly the merchants who wanted to lobby for lucrative army contracts. Frémont also ran afoul of the powerful and wealthy Blair family, who were the leading political power in the state. He refused to grant a large supply contract to a close friend of the Blairs, and then declined to appoint Francis Blair' son Frank Jr. as a Major General.

Frémont's greatest comflict with the Missourians was over the explosive issue of slavery. He was an ardent abolitionist in a state where slavery was an important part of the economic system. His lack of sensitivity to local and even national concerns became apparent in a proclamation he issued on 30 August 1861 whereby he assumed the administrative powers of the state in order to suppress disorder and maintain public peace. In this proclamation he declared martial law and promised to confiscate all property of those in rebellion, including slaves: "The property, real and personal, of all persons in the State of Missouri who shall take up arms against the United States, or who shall be directly proven to have taken an active part with their enemies in the field, is declared to be confiscated to the public use, and their slaves, if any they have, are hereby declared freemen."

This clause was quite an embarrassment to President Lincoln, who was doing everything in his power to keep Missouri and the other slave holding border states of Kentucky, Maryland and Delaware, in the Union. He realized that the emancipation issue was sure to drive these states away, and requested Frémont to modify his proclamation. When Frémont refused to do so, the President had to cancel Frémont's emancipation order himself.

This emancipation issue brought the end of Frémont's tenure as commander of the Western Department, which had already been shaken by the Union loss at the battle of Wilson's Creek on 10 August. Because of Frémont's political influence, it took Lincoln almost three months to replace him. When he was finally relieved of duty on 2 November, Frémont was kept in limbo for four months. He was then reassigned to a seemingly out of the way sector of the war—the Mountain Department of western Virginia, where he assumed command on 29 March 1862, just in time to run right into Stonewall Jackson's whirlwind Valley Campaign. The inept Frémont was

no match for Jackson, and saw his troops lose the battles of McDowell and Cross Keys; Frémont's slow approach to Strasburg on 27 May was largely responsible for Jackson's escape from the trap designed by Lincoln to snare Stonewall in the lower Valley.

After the Valley Campaign, Frémont's command was reassigned to become the *I Corps* of John Pope's *Army of Virginia*. Frémont refused to serve under Pope, since he technically outranked his newly assigned army commander, so he resigned on 28 June 1862. This was fine with Pope and everyone in Washington. Frémont spent the rest of the war "on the bench" waiting for a new assignment that never came.

Frémont's later adventures included being a radical Republican candidate for President in 1864. He then turned to railroad speculation, and in 1873 was convicted of fraud in France for his role in a scheme to build a transcontinental railroad from San Francisco to Norfolk. Frémont also served as governor of Arizona from 1878 to 1881.

CHAPTER V

Jackson Moves North

20–25 May 1862

*I*t was a pleasant spring day when Jackson's men resumed their interrupted march from New Market on 20 May. From New Market, they turned east through the gap in the Massanutten Mountains into the Luray Valley and then followed Ewell north. The troops marched well, making at times 30 miles a day and earning for themselves the sobriquet "Jackson's foot cavalry." Not one to waste any time, Jackson reorganized his command while on the march. His own division—the Stonewall Brigade (now under Brig. Gen. Charles S. Winder) and Campbell's and Taliaferro's brigades, plus Ashby's cavalry—remained under his own direct control. Johnson's command was reorganized and absorbed into Ewell's division, since Johnson's foot wound at McDowell forced him to withdraw from the campaign: Col. W.C. Scott's 2nd Brigade (44th, 52nd and 58th Virginia) was absorbed intact into Ewell's division, and the 2nd Brigade (12th Georgia and 25th and 31st Virginia) was joined with Jackson's 13th Virginia to form a new brigade under Brig. Gen. Arnold Elzey. Ewell's other two brigades were crack troops. Taylor's Louisiana brigade (6th, 7th, 8th, and 9th regiments plus the Louisiana Tigers) was a first class outfit, and Brig. Gen. Isaac Trimble (commanding the 21st North Carolina, 21st Georgia, 15th Alabama, and 16th Mississippi) was a first class fighter. A final but significant change was the creation of a demi-brigade called the "Maryland Line" commanded by Brig. Gen. George

During the Valley Campaign Brig. Gen. George H. "Maryland" Steuart commanded one of Jackson's cavalry brigades and then a provisional brigade called the "Maryland Line."

"Maryland" Steuart. This unit, consisting of the 1st Maryland infantry plus Company A, Capt. J.R. Brown's company of Maryland cavalry, and Capt. J. B. Brockenbrough's Baltimore battery, was formed to assert Maryland's status as one of the Confederate states and stress her contribution to the cause, and incidently to increase recruiting. The Maryland Line was attached to Ewell's command, as were the 2nd and 6th Virginia Cavalry Regiments. Altogether, Jackson's two divisions composed 17,000 experienced men and 50 guns, a strong and determined force for the Federals to reckon with.

On 22 May the Confederate force sneaked down the Luray Valley with the goal of overwhelming Col. John R. Kenly's small Union garrison at Front Royal. Ewell's division led the way, followed by Jackson's. Stonewall sent his cavalry, under Ashby and Flournoy, to destroy the rail and telegraph lines between Front Royal and Strasburg so that Banks could not reinforce Kenly from Strasburg. Once this goal was accomplished, Flour-

Brig. Gen. Dick Ewell was Jackson's second-in-command during the height of the Valley Campaign. He had a wooden leg as a result of a previous wound and had to be strapped to his horse to keep from falling off.

noy was to take his cavalry and approach Front Royal from the west, so as to intercept any of Kenly's men who might retreat in that direction.

Col. Turner Ashby's 7th Virginia Cavalry was up at dawn to carry out their part of Jackson's strategy. At midmorning they sneaked into Buckton Station, a key stop on the Manassas Gap Railroad halfway between Strasburg and Front Royal. In less than five minutes of wild fighting Ashby took possession of the station, and then headed for Front Royal. Meanwhile, Col. Thomas S. Flournoy's 2nd and 6th Virginia Cavalry Regiments had also cut the railroad between Buckton Station and Front Royal. Meanwhile, another small cavalry detachment was sent toward Strasburg, where it put up quite a front, threatening the town all evening and through the night.

Front Royal, 23 May 1862

With Front Royal isolated, Jackson began his primary attack, approaching from the south. Spearheading his advance were the 1st Maryland and the Louisiana Tigers, supported by the remainder of Taylor's brigade. Fighting began about 1400, when the Confederate advance guard ran into Kenly's pickets one and one-half miles south of Front Royal. Altogether Kenly had only

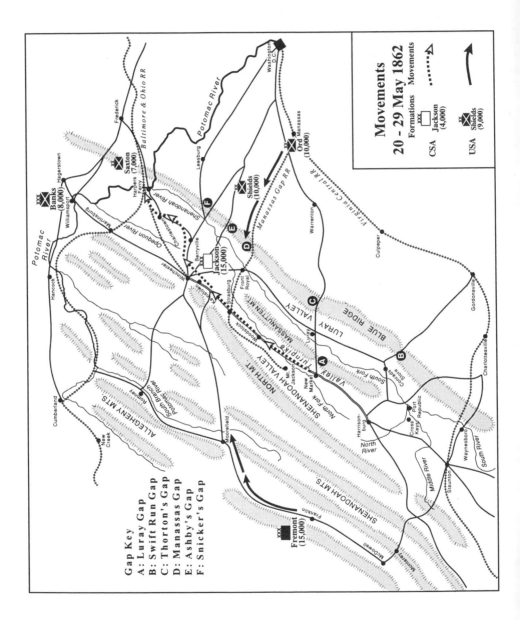

Movements
20 - 29 May 1862

Gap Key
A: Luray Gap
B: Swift Run Gap
C: Thorton's Gap
D: Manassas Gap
E: Ashby's Gap
F: Snicker's Gap

twelve companies of infantry—nine from his own Union *1st Maryland Regiment*, two from the *29th Pennsylvania*, and one of pioneers—plus two 10–pounder Parrott guns with which to face Jackson. Kenly posted two companies to support his pickets, and kept one in Front Royal. Another six companies were encamped on Richardson's Hill, on the Front Royal side of the key bridge over the Shenandoah, a structure the Yankees had rebuilt after it was destroyed by Jackson in March. Of Kenly's three remaining companies, one was guarding the Manassas Gap Railroad, east of Front Royal, and two were guarding the railroad bridges over the North and South Forks of the Shenandoah.

It did not take Jackson's troops long to drive back Kenly's pickets and their supports. Soon the Confederates held possession of the town, as the surviving Federals joined the remainder of Kenly's command on Richardson's Hill. Here the Union line was strengthened by two companies of the *5th New York Cavalry Regiment*, which happened then to arrive from the west. When Kenly's rifled guns opened fire, Jackson had to slow down because he had no rifled artillery to repress them. The first battery that had come up was short ranged and so could not reach the Union position, causing the irate Jackson to sit and wait for rifled guns to come up.

Jackson, however, was not one to sit still while he waited. He sent the 6th Virginia to the left and ordered the Tigers and Confederate 1st Maryland to charge straight against the enemy. Kenly and his command fought valiantly for an hour in a hot little action which pitted Yankee Marylanders against Rebel ones. Then, when he saw his position become hopeless as Flournoy's cavalrymen began approaching his right rear, Kenly set fire to his camp and ordered his men to run for it across the two Shenandoah bridges. Kenly tried to burn the roadway bridge over the South Fork, but failed. Nevertheless, if he succeeded in burning the North Fork bridge, he would get clean away and Jackson would be unable to advance any farther. Jackson's heart leaped when he saw flames licking the timbers of the North Fork bridge. Without hesitation, he ordered Taylor's men to seize the bridge and save it. Taylor later wrote, "It was rather a near thing-my horse and clothing were scorched

Flournoy's cavalrymen skirmish with some New York troopers near Front Royal while cutting the railroad to Buckton Station.

and many men burned their hands severely while throwing brands into the river."

With the bridge saved, Jackson tried to rush his men after Kenly. But he grew angered to see many of his troops (including the Louisiana Tigers) lingering in Front Royal to loot the captured Yankee camps; in addition, most of Ashby's cavalry had dispersed or taken after a Union supply train from the east that had the bad luck to arrive in town at that moment. To make matters worse, Jackson's reserves were slow coming up.

Stonewall nevertheless pressed on with about 250 cavalry from Flournoy's command. About three miles north of Front Royal Flournoy met and defeated Kenly's rear guard, the two companies of the *5th New York Cavalry*. When Kenly saw this, he stopped his infantry column and ordered it to turn and form facing the enemy. But Jackson and Flournoy were not to be stopped, despite odds of four-to-one against them. The Confederate cavalry made a mounted charge directly against Kenly's infantry. Company B of Flournoy's own 6th Virginia Cavalry charged directly up the turnpike, supported by Company E on its left and Companies A and K on its right. Kenly's men were in no mood to face charging cavalry. Their line disintegrated, and Kenly fell wounded while trying to reform his men. Flournoy's cavalry pursued the fugitives almost all the way to Winchester, hauling in numerous captives every mile. Jackson's victory was complete.

Union casualties at Front Royal amounted to 90 percent of Kenly's force-32 killed, 122 wounded, and 750 captured; less than 150 of Kenly's men escaped to report for duty the next day. Jackson's total losses amounted to only 36 killed and wounded. It had indeed been a glorious victory. But to Jackson it was only a prelude of greater things to come. His goal was to eliminate Banks' command. However, he would not know exactly how to do this until he ascertained Banks' response to the Front Royal fight. Clearly, Banks had to be intercepted before he reached Winchester. If the Confederates moved their whole force to Winchester, there was the distinct danger that Banks might escape east via Front Royal. To forestall this, Jackson directed his men to head for Middletown, four miles north of Strasburg. From there they would be able to intercept Banks no matter which direction the Yankees went, north or east.

The Race to Winchester, 23–25 May 1862

On his part, Banks at first was quite confused about the events at Front Royal. When the communications between Strasburg and Front Royal were cut at mid-day on the 23rd, Banks assumed that this was due to some sort of cavalry raid. He discounted Kenly's claims that a vastly superior enemy force was approaching Front Royal, but nevertheless sent a few reinforcements to shore up Kenly's spirit. Some of these (the two companies of the *5th New York Cavalry* already mentioned) arrived in time to assist Kenly; a force of infantry dispatched later was halted by part of Ashby's cavalry at Buckton Station.

Major General Nathaniel P. Banks was defeated by Jackson at 1st Winchester and Cedar Mountain, but won the thanks of Congress for his capture of Port Hudson, Louisiana, in July 1863.

When Banks received definite news that Kenly's command had been smashed by an enemy force of 15,000 or more, he knew he was in a pickle. He had no choice but to leave Strasburg, since he would surely be surrounded and captured if he stayed there. There were three basic choices open to Banks—to retreat north through the mountains to the Potomac, to attack the enemy at Front Royal, or to make a dash for Winchester. Banks dismissed the first alternative because it would force him to abandon his trains, and he eliminated the second because he thought Jackson's command was too large to engage in open combat. "It was therefore determined," Banks later wrote, "to enter the lists with the enemy in a race, or battle, as he should choose, for the possession of Winchester, the key of the valley, and for us the position of safety."

Banks had his troops up soon after dawn on 24 May, and they were on the march by 0900. They were led by Col. Dudley Donnelly's *1st Brigade* in the front, followed by Col. George H. Gordon's *3rd Brigade*. Meanwhile, John P. Hatch was with all the cavalry and six cannons. Banks was still misreading the situation and believed that only a part of Jackson's force had attacked Kenly at Front Royal. As a result, Hatch went south looking for Jackson, who was thought to be approaching from Woodstock, rather than north, towards safety. However, it was not long before Hatch reported no Confederates were in front of him. Banks then realized his error and recalled Hatch, who thus had a late start in the race to Winchester.

To ascertain Banks' movements, early on the 24th Jackson sent Brig. Gen. "Maryland" Steuart with the 2nd and 6th Virginia Cavalry Regiments to Newtown, nine miles south of Winchester and about as many miles north of Strasburg. Steuart was to report immediately if Banks was or was not that far on his way to Winchester—intelligence that Jackson sorely needed. If the bulk of Banks' force was already beyond Newtown, Jackson had no chance of intercepting the Yankees before they reached Winchester; if Banks was not in the area, then he could still be intercepted, provided that he had not headed in a different direction. Possibilities for Banks' action seemed endless that day, and Jackson was doing the proper thing to investigate the options that seemed most likely.

Putting Steuart in charge of the reconnoitering cavalry detachment was a stroke of genius—Steuart had served in the U.S. Regular Cavalry before the war, and was an experienced and reliable man for such a mission. While Steuart carried out his mission, Jackson marched his infantry only part way towards Winchester. His troops had gotten a late start that morning, and it took them quite a while to cross the partially damaged Shenandoah River bridges. In addition, Stonewall was reluctant to advance too far north for fear that Banks might strike at Front Royal. For these reasons, Jackson halted his infantry for an early lunch, with the head of the column at Ninevah and the tail at Cedarville.

Jackson then spent an anxious morning waiting for news from Steuart. At 1100 he finally heard the report he wanted. When Steuart reached Newtown, he discovered a passing Union wagon train. A quick charge scattered the alarmed Yankees, who retreated back on Banks' main column. When Banks received news that Confederate cavalry was at Middletown, he sent Donnelly's brigade forward to clear the way, and ordered Hatch to come up in support. By the time Donnelly and the *1st Michigan Cavalry* chased Steuart off and cleared the road, the Yankees had lost an hour of marching time. Banks realized his predicament and ordered his men to remove their knapsacks so they could march faster.

As soon as he received Steuart's report, Jackson understood that Banks' command was strung out on the road from Strasburg to Winchester and so could be caught and smashed. Stonewall at once set his infantry in motion towards Middletown. By noon his weary men were toiling through light rain and over muddy roads. Despite Stonewall's proddings, it took them over three hours to reach their destination.

At about 1530 Jackson's advance reached Middletown, and found the road thronged with Banks' men and wagons in both directions. Jackson had taken the foresight to send Chew's and Poague's batteries with his vanguard, and the artillerymen had a field day. Artillerist George Neese described the scene: "At a half mile range, we opened up on the flying mixture with all of our guns, and as our shells plowed gap after gap through the serried column it caused consternation confounded, and vastly increased the speed of the mixed fugitive mass."

While his cannons were popping away, Jackson threw Ashby's cavalry and Taylor's infantry into the confused mass at Middletown. Jackson himself described the scene as follows: "The road was literally obstructed with the mingled and confused mass of struggling and dying horses and riders. The Federal column was pierced, but what proportion of its strength had passed north towards Winchester I had no means of knowing. Among the surviving cavalry the wildest confusion ensued, and they scattered in disorder in various directions, leaving, however, some two hundred prisoners with their equipments in our hands. A train of wagons was seen disappearing in the distance towards Winchester, and Ashby, with his cavalry, some artillery, and a supporting infantry force from Taylor's brigade, was sent in pursuit."

It turned out that Jackson had smashed into Hatch's cavalry command. The confused and frightened Yankees fled in all directions—some by a circuitous route to Winchester, others withdrawing to Strasburg. The *5th New York Cavalry* kept on running until it reached Clear Spring, Maryland, on the other side of the Potomac, which it crossed accompanied by 32 wagons and a goodly number of stragglers.

Though Jackson now held a strong position at Middletown, he was for a long time uncertain if Banks' infantry had yet passed by there on its way to Winchester. When Union artillery appeared south of Middletown and formed up, Jackson moved his infantry to face them. Much to his dismay, the Yankees then gave up their bold front, limbered up, and headed north by back roads. By now Jackson realized that the bulk of Banks' command was north of Middletown, not south. He had wasted two hours at Middletown, and his forced march had been for nothing.

Banks had indeed been lucky to make it to Winchester at all. He may have lost several hundred prisoners and stragglers, and much of his cavalry and artillery may have been dispersed all over the countryside, but at least he still had most of his infantry intact. He had escaped so far partly because of his quick decision to march out of Strasburg, but his escape was due more

Civil War units were often obstructed by their own supply trains.

to the weariness of Jackson's troops and Stonewall's own indecision at Middletown. Also of help was the fact that the numerous broken down and abandoned Union supply wagons delayed the Confederate advance by sidetracking many looters, particularly Ashby's undisciplined cowboys. These wagons were also physically blocking the road at many points.

To defend Winchester, Banks had only about 6400 men, well under half of Jackson's strength. He placed Gordon's *3rd Brigade* on his right, on a series of hills immediately west of town. These hills continued southwest past the hills Jackson had been aiming to occupy; still farther south they became the same broad ridge on which Garnett had been defeated at the Battle of Kernstown. Gordon posted the *2nd Massachusetts* on his right, and the *3rd Wisconsin* on his left, near the turnpike; a battery of six guns supported the line, and the *27th Indiana* and *29th Pennsylvania* were held in reserve. The center of Banks' line, at the point where the Valley Turnpike entered Winchester, was held by Hatch's cavalry and two cannon. On the left, Banks put Donnelly's *1st Brigade*, which, aided by eight artillery pieces, guarded the Front Royal road. Banks was well aware that his men were tired, dispirited, and outnumbered. Apparently he stayed to fight because he feared his army would disintegrate if he tried to disengage from an active enemy so close to his front.

While Jackson was being frustrated at Middletown, Steuart and Ewell were having more luck at keeping contact with the enemy. Steuart followed the Union column slowly until he was checked at Newtown by the *28th New York* and *2nd Massachusetts* of Gordon's *3rd Brigade*, which were soon reinforced by the remnants of Hatch's cavalry. This Union rear guard held until dark, when Jackson's arrival from Middletown and Ewell's advance on the Front Royal road persuaded Hatch and Gordon to withdraw. The two left behind Lieutenant Col. George L. Andrews and his *2nd Massachusetts* as a rear guard, and Andrews did a marvelous job blocking Jackson's advance.

Stonewall was most anxious to overrun the impertinent Yankees and seize the high ground southwest of Winchester before dawn. His men, though, were too tired to accomplish the mission. Jackson selected the Stonewall Brigade and began pushing forward in the darkness. Once, then twice, his men walked into ambushes. The handful of Ashby's cavalry who were with the advance—most were absent or drunk from their pillaging earlier in the day—bolted when they were ordered to charge. Their stampeding horses almost trampled Capt. William T. Poague's artillerymen and the 33rd Virginia. Many men of the 2nd and 5th Virginia Regiments were skittish after an ammunition wagon exploded, and when they ran into an open field they were shot at by their own men who thought they were the enemy. In spite of these difficulties, Jackson was determined to press on. Finally at 0200 Colonel Fulkerson pleaded for some rest for his men and Jackson reluctantly granted them two hours. The weary infantrymen then literally dropped where they stood. Jackson himself reportedly stayed up all night, alone, planning the coming battle.

Winchester, 25 May 1862

Jackson's orders for 25 May—another Sabbath day battle—were simple and straightforward: "Attack at dawn." At sunup he sent Winder's 1st Brigade forward to seize the hills southwest of Winchester; he deemed these were necessary to hold in order to control the course of the battle. Curiously, no Federals were posted there. Jackson then proceeded to form his entire division, reinforced by Taylor's fine 8th Brigade, in a battle line that would soon smash into Banks' army from the southwest.

Meanwhile, the day's fighting had already been started by Ewell southeast of town. At dawn he sent forward Col. Bradley T. Johnson's Rebel 1st Maryland as skirmishers. It was so foggy that Johnson lost contact with his own lines as well as those of the enemy; he then prudently withdrew to an orchard and waited for the fog to burn off. Ewell, who was never noted for his patience, then sent the 21st North Carolina forward to locate the Union lines. This unfortunate regiment ran right into devastating enemy volleys from the *5th Connecticut* and *46th Pennsylvania*. Lieutenant Col. George Chapman of the *5th Connecticut* later described the action: "About five o'clock Sunday morning, as the men were rising from their sleep and heating their coffee in the field which we entered late the night before, a shell suddenly fell amongst them. This was followed by others in rapid succession. The men quickly seized their muskets and fell into line as calmly as if on parade. . . . The enemy's infantry soon appeared on the hill in front, charging directly upon us. Companies A and F immediately moved forward beyond the fence and delivered their fire with effect upon the enemy, now within a few rods. The whole battalion then moved up to their line, and, delivering three well-directed volleys, mowed down the enemy in scores, shooting away their flag each time. At the third volley Companies I and B delivered a cross fire by a half-wheel to the right. The enemy broke and ran in confusion."

The quick repulse of the 21st North Carolina taught Ewell a bloody lesson. Instead of another frontal attack, he decided it would be wiser to try to outflank the opposing enemy line. Accordingly, he sent the 1st Maryland to work its way around the Federal right, and the 21st Georgia to do the same to the enemy left. Meanwhile, he began blasting the Union center with his artillery. When both the 1st Maryland and 21st Georgia worked their way around his flanks, Donnelly had no choice but to withdraw to a line closer to Winchester.

Meanwhile the fighting was extended to Jackson's flank. Colonel Gordon had seen Jackson's troops deploying, and extended his own line farther to the west in order to meet this challenge. Gordon's artillery, supported by the *2nd Massachusetts*, soon was giving Poague's artillerymen such trouble that Poague had to shift his position to the rear. In response, Jackson sent Colonel Campbell to extend Winder's line to the west. Campbell's men were then reinforced by Taliaferro, but still the Yankee artillery kept banging away. In fact, the Federal line grew stronger as Gordon shifted the *27th Indiana* and *29th Pennsylvania* to his right.

At this juncture, Jackson brought up his new shock troops, Taylor's Louisiana brigade. Taylor was busting his buttons with pride to be given this post of honor. As some of his men ducked to avoid enemy artillery shells, he yelled out, "What the hell are you dodging for? If there is any more of it, you will be halted under this fire for an hour." The Louisianians stopped in their tracks, as fearful of Taylor's outburst as they were of Jackson's response—for Stonewall had been in earshot of Taylor's blast,

Stonewall Jackson was riding his favorite mount, Little Sorrel, when he was mortally wounded at Chancellorsville on 2 May 1863.

and "Old Blue Light" never condoned cursing, especially on the Sabbath. Jackson, ever laconic, just told Taylor, "I am afraid you are a wicked fellow," and then turned to another part of the line.

Taylor now led his brigade to the far left of Jackson's line in preparation for his attack on Banks' left. From there he mounted a textbook charge, with 3000 Louisianians keeping perfect order as they advanced steadily in close order, pausing occasionally to realign after crossing hollows or fences. Col. George H. Gordon, commander of the line that Taylor was attacking said, "Three large battalions of infantry, moving in order of battle, came out from their cover and approached my brigade. They were re-

Brig. Gen. Isaac R. Trimble was the excellent commander of Ewell's 7th Brigade.

ceived with a destructive fire of musketry, poured in from all parts of my line that could reach them. Confident in their numbers and relying upon larger sustaining bodies (suspicions of which behind the covering timbers in our front were surely confirmed), the enemy's lines moved on, but little shaken by our fire."

Shortly after Taylor began his charge he was supported by Winder's brigade. Gordon observed, "At the same time, in our front, a long line of infantry showed themselves, rising the crest of the hills just beyond our position. My little brigade, numbering in all just 2102, in another moment might have been overwhelmed. On its right, left and center immensely superior columns were pressing. Not another man was available; not a support to be found in the remnant of his army corps left General Banks."

Just as this Confederate attack on the left was cresting, Trimble's 7th Brigade, of Ewell's division, was breaking Donnelly's *1st Brigade* southeast of Winchester. Everywhere the

Banks' Union troops retreat across the Potomac after their defeat at Winchester. They left behind so many supplies that Jackson's men called the defeated Union commander "Commissary Banks."

whole Union line collapsed at once. Jackson himself got carried away with elation as he shouted "Let's holler! Order forward the whole army to the Potomac!"

Colonel Gordon described the situation on his front, "On every side above the surrounding crest surged the rebel forces. A sharp and withering fire of musketry was opened by the enemy from the crest upon our center, left and right. The yells of a victorious and merciless foe were above the din of battle. . .Gordon had to order a retreat. It soon became a rout: "My retreating column suffered serious loss in the streets of Winchester. Males and females vied with each other in increasing the number of their victims, by firing from the houses, throwing hand grenades, hot water, and missiles of every description. The hellish spirit of murder was carried on by the enemy's cavalry, who followed to butcher, and who struck down with saber and pistol the hapless soldier."

Following its defeat at Winchester, Maj. Gen. Banks' Union division did not rally until it safely crossed the Potomac. It later recrossed at Williamsport but could not move fast enough to catch Jackson, who was rushing south in order to escape being trapped by Frémont and Ord.

Banks' troops retreated hastily through the bedlam in Winchester and streamed north towards Martinsburg, leaving behind numerous wounded, prisoners, and sick. A few of the Yankees tried to make a stand in Winchester's town square, but they were outflanked and routed by Winder's 5th Virginia. All Jackson needed to complete his victory was for his cavalry to sweep up the remains of the enemy army. But Ashby and his men were nowhere to be seen. It seems that Ashby had taken the remnants of his force-many still hung over from their pillaging the previous day-and headed towards Berryville to intercept any Federals in that quarter. He did not return until well after Banks' force had fled to Martinsburg. Nor could Jackson get any help from Steuart's cavalry force. Steuart, still commanding the 2nd and 6th Virginia Cavalry Regiments, delayed matters considerably by refusing to obey an order from Sandie Pendleton of Jackson's staff because it did not come through Ewell.

Meanwhile, the impatient Jackson improvised a small cavalry force by mounting artillerymen on caisson horses. These make-do troopers captured several hundred Yankees, but were neither armed nor organized properly to pursue Banks' confused masses very far.

Jackson was well aware of the opportunity for a complete and total victory which he was missing. When he wrote his battle report later, he stated, "Never have I seen an opportunity when it was in the power of cavalry to reap a richer harvest of the fruits of victory. Hoping that cavalry would soon come up, the artillery, followed by infantry, was pressed forward for about two hours for the purpose of preventing, by artillery fire, a reforming of the enemy; but as nothing was heard of the cavalry, and as but little or nothing could be accomplished without it in the exhausted condition of our infantry, between whom and the enemy the distance was continually increasing, I ordered a halt, and issued orders for going into camp and refreshing the men."

Yet, Jackson's victory had been quite thorough, even by his own exacting standards. At a cost of 400 casualties he had reduced Banks' army to a disorganized mass fleeing toward the Potomac. All together Banks lost over 3500 men, more than half his force, plus over 9000 weapons, piles of supplies, and tons of provisions. The latter were so plentiful that many of Jackson's men took to calling General Banks "Commissary Banks" because of the generous provisions he supplied them at this time.

Belle Boyd

One reason for Jackson's great success in the Valley Campaign was his intelligence gathering. His main sources for information about the enemy were Ashby's cavalry and the friendly natives of the Valley. Another key source was 18–year-old "Belle" Boyd, one of the South's most famous spies. She was a native of the lower Valley, and used her wit and vivacity to gather information and pass it on to Southern leaders, particularly Jackson. One of her most famous exploits was before the Battle of Front Royal. As Jackson and his troops were approaching to attack the town on 23 May 1862, she rode out to the army at full speed to tell Jackson the disposition of the town's Union defenders and what their intentions were. Her report helped Jackson to victory that day.

Because of her flamboyant personality, Belle had trouble keeping her occupation a secret. At one point Union general James Shields, perhaps Jackson's most competent adversary in the Valley, had to warn her to keep a lower profile or he would have to deal sternly with her. Belle nonetheless did not slow down; by the time she was 21 she

had been arrested numerous times and imprisoned twice. Even then she did not stop her spying—supposedly, when she was being held in Washington's Old Capitol Prison, she sent messages inside rubber balls she threw out the window. Northern authorities did not know quite what to make of her in those Victorian times; all they did was warn her frequently and send her back to the Confederate lines with admonitions to behave.

Belle's personal habits also affronted Southern women, who were embarrassed by her brazenness and her alleged unseemly methods of getting information from Yankee officers. This did not bother Belle or prevent her from continuing her wild ways. In 1863 she carried personal dispatches from Jefferson Davis to England, where she became an instant success as a stage personality. After the war closed she wrote her dramatic memoirs, *Belle Boyd in Camp and Prison*, and went on the lecture circuit, constantly embellishing her escapades. She was on such a tour when she died of a heart attack in Wisconsin in 1900 at age 57.

The Baltimore and Ohio Railroad

During his Valley Campaign, Jackson made war as much on the Baltimore and Ohio Railroad as he did on the Federal troops. He knew that the railroad, whose main line passed through Harpers Ferry on its

way from Baltimore to Wheeling, was a key transportation line that brought coal and other raw materials from Western Virginia to the Washington area, as well as troops and supplies from Ohio and the

Midwest. Each time he could interrupt service or damage the busy B & O line, he forced backups to occur to the west as well as an overload on the Pennsylvania Central Railroad, which ran east from Ohio through Pittsburgh and Harrisburg.

The B & O was chartered in 1827 and was financed largely by investors in Baltimore for the purpose of exploiting trade with the interior and preventing Baltimore from being eclipsed as a trading port by Philadelphia and New York. Construction of the line proved awkward beyond western Maryland, because permission had to be secured from Virginia to pass through her western counties (which would become the State of West Virginia in 1863). Virginia's businessmen were not eager to see the B & O run directly to Cincinnati, as the Marylanders wished, because they had their ownn plans to do trade in that direction. As a result, the builders of the B & O were only given permission to build a terminus at Wheeling, which was awkwardly close to the Pennsylvania Central's westward terminus at Steubenville.

When the Civil War began, the B & O had 513 miles of tracks, only about one third of which was actually in Maryland. The main line ran westward from Baltimore past Monocacy Junction to Harpers Ferry (Va), whence it continued into Cumberland and then to Grafton (WVa) before ending at Wheeling (Va). Because of the lay of the land along the Potomac River, most of the line between Harpers Ferry and Cumberland ran on the Virginia side of the river, a situation that would cause much tension at the beginning of the war, as will be seen. The railroad also had three significant side branches in 1861: One line ran from Grafton to Parkersburg through the coal country of western Virginia, and a second line ran from Harper's Ferry to Winchester. The third and most important side branch ran from the Relay House near Baltimore to Washington, and was the capital's only rail link with the North.

The wealth of the B & O in 1861 can be seen from its vast holdings in machinery, which included 236 locomotives, and 3579 passenger and freight cars, as well as all the stations, roundhouses, and repair shops needed to run the line, not to mention numerous costly trestles, bridges and tunnels.

The creation of the Confederacy put the B & O in a very awkward and sensitive position, since its tracks ran through two slave holding states. The railroad received intense pressure from the Federal government to transport troops and supplies to Washington, but Virginia (which had not yet seceded) and the people of eastern Maryland were not willing for this to happen. Garrett Smith, the president of the B & O, tried to walk a tightrope but was unable to placate both opposing parties. Freight traffic dropped badly as shippers feared a possible interruption to the line and switched to routes farther north. Affairs came to a head on 19 April 1861 when a mob in Baltimore rioted while the *6th Massachusetts* infantry was passing through on its way to Washington, and both soldiers and civilians were killed. The situation was so tense there that Federal authorities decided to develop an alternate route by sea to

Annapolis; from there a sidespur line connected to the B & O's Washington branch south of Baltimore at Annapolis Junction.

The B & O's position became even more precarious as Virginia inched closer to secession (which finally came on 23 May). The railroad line would run squarely through the cockpit of the war and would be subject to the depredations of both sides. And the railroad's principal enemy during the first year and a half of the war would be none other than Stonewall Jackson.

As noted in Chapter 1, Jackson was made Confederate commander at Winchester on 27 April 1861. By threatening to shut down the B & O, he forced the railroad to run all its traffic through Harpers Ferry between 1100 and 1300 each day beginning 15 May. For a week this stretch of line became the busiest railroad on the continent during those hours. Then on 22 May he closed down both ends of the railroad track near Harpers Ferry, and craftily captured 56 engines and 300 cars. The problem for him, though, was that he had nowhere to transfer his prizes, since the railroad line ran no farther south than Winchester. When McClellan's successful campaign secured most of western Virginia (including the B & O's branch line from Grafton to Parkersburg) for the Union, Jackson found that he had to withdraw from Harpers Ferry. As a result he was forced to burn his captured locomotives on 23 May. Jackson's immense destruction of the B & O's private property helped crystallize the owners of the railroad, as well as considerable public opinion in Baltimore, against the Confederacy.

From this point on, Northern military authorities as well as the railroad's managers, spent considerable resources and effort to keep the B & O open. Secretary of War Edwin M. Stanton was particularly interested in using the railroad to bring supplies and troops to Washington; the ability to do so also entailed control of all Maryland and much of northern and western Virginia. Railroad historian Festus P. Summers even argues that the recovery of the B & O's line was a war aim second ony to the opening of the Mississippi River.

Over the winter of 1861-62 Jackson spent considerable effort trying to break up the B & O Railroad from his base at Winchester. His December expedition against the railroad and Dam No. 5 of the Chesapeake and Ohio Canal is described in the text. His destruction of the railroad line consisted primarily of stealing the rails and burning the cross ties.

Jackson was forced to evacuate Winchester on 11 March 1862, and strenuous Union effort had the railroad back in operation on 29 March. There was such a backup of freight at Cumberland and Grafton that 3800 freight cars passed through Harpers Ferry on 30 March. Jackson was not able to assault the B & O line again until two months later, following his victory at Winchester on 25 May. However, he was soon forced to withdraw, and was able to destroy only two railroad bridges near Martinsburg.

The railroad resumed operations for four months until Lee began his first invasion of the north, culminating in the battle of Antietam. During the campaign, Jackson captured a large garrison at Harpers Ferry and Confederate troops destroyed the railroad line and its associated buildings for a distance of 35 miles from Harpers Ferry to Back Creek. This damage could not be repaired until the Confederates were pushed out of Winchester in November. The owners of the B & O then repaired the broken section of the line using rails and ties that they had been stockpiling in order to build a second line of tracks along their very lucrative Washington Branch.

The railroad reopened its main branch on 1 January 1863, but would still suffer frequent depredations before the end of the war. "Grumble" Jones and John Imboden conducted a lengthy and successful raid against the western branches of the railroad, especially in the Grafton area, in April 1863. The railroad was reopened on 4 May, only to be closed again by Lee's Gettysburg invasion from 17 June to the end of July, which destroyed 7 miles of track and numerous supporting structures and bridges near Harpers Ferry. Once again , the line was repaired with ties and rails that had been stockpiled, to construct a second line between Baltimore and Washington.

Union defense of the railroad line became more effective with the development of block houses and armored cars, but the North never had enough garrisons to control the countryside and guard the railroad line continually against raiders like Harry Gilmore (who struck the line in February 1862) and John S. Mosby (who could cut the railroad any time he wished, most notably in

his "Greenback Raid" in October 1864). Nor did the North place enough importance on the lower Shenandoah to be able to stop Jubal Early from breaking up the line during his July 1864 invasion of Maryland. Railroad officials worked feverishly to reopen the line on 26 July, only to see Early cut it again in September and October.

It was not until late 1864 that the North sent an aggressive commander to the lower Valley with a strong enough force to control the area and give real protection to the most vulnerable section of the B & O line. Previous commanders in this district, which underwent a number of changes in designation, had never been particularly strong— Robert Patterson, John C. Frémont and Franz Sigel were not overly able, and Robert Schenck and Benjamin Kelley commanded in the area while recovering from battle wounds. This all changed on 6 August 1864 when Major General Philip M. Sheridan took command of an enlarged command entitled the Middle Military Division, with specific orders and enough troops to take control of the Valley and secure the B & O's rail line for good.

In the end, the B & O survived the war, despite its precarious location in the cockpit of the action. It may even have been stronger in 1865 than in 1861 due to the profits gained from its monopoly on the critical Baltimore to Washington line, and the Federal government's military and financial support of the railroad's main line to Wheeling. There is no question that the B & O aided the Union cause materially during the war, despite the efforts of Stonewall Jackson, and numerous other Confederate generals and raiders, to put it out of action. Another less appreciated contribution by the B & O was its role in the creation of the state of West Virginia out of the nucleus of Western Virginia counties served by its main line and its Grafton to Parkersburg branch. Specifically, it is very unlikely that West Virginia's six most eastern counties (Pendleton, Hardy, Hampshire, Morgan, Berkeley, and Jefferson) would have seceded from Virginia had it not been for the influence of the B & O's main line, which passed through them or nearby.

CHAPTER VI

March and Countermarch

26 May–7 June 1862

*J*ackson's May offensive, culminating in his victory at Winchester had been brilliant. He had been more successful than he hoped. Indeed, he had perhaps been dangerously successful. His attack on Banks focused the attention on his theatre of operations. More importantly, Jackson's success brought President Lincoln a determination to do away with Stonewall Jackson once and for all.

Lincoln Lays a Trap

So far Lincoln's conduct of the war had seemed to be going pretty well. George McClellan was inching along the Peninsula towards Richmond, where he had Joe Johnston's army pinned down, and Irvin McDowell was poised at Fredericksburg to advance against token opposition and deliver the decisive blow to the Rebel capital. The only uncertainty in the Union plans was the location and intention of Jackson's force, which had not really been heard from since it left the Valley town of McDowell in early May.

When he first heard the news of the engagement at Front Royal, Lincoln, like Banks, thought it was merely a cavalry raid. As a precaution, however, the President directed McDowell to leave an additional brigade (the one he judged "least effective") at Fredericksburg before advancing south towards Richmond.

Frémont's vanguard arrives at Strasburg too late to cut off Jackson's retreat. All they could do was to watch Jackson's trains head south toward Fisher's Hill.

As more dire news came from the Valley, Lincoln was forced to rethink the entire strategic situation. On 24 May Banks had reported that Ewell had taken Front Royal and Jackson was pressing forward from Strasburg. Other rumors placed Jackson east to the Blue Ridge and perhaps even marching on Washington itself. Lincoln did not waste time making a decision. He figured that Jackson's rear must be vulnerable no matter whether Stonewall were at Strasburg or farther east. Accordingly, at 1600 on the 24th he directed General Frémont to suspend his proposed march on Knoxville and proceed instead from Franklin northwestwards to the Valley: "The exposed condition of General Banks makes his immediate relief a point of paramount importance. You are therefore ordered by the President to move against Jackson at Harrisonburg and operate against the enemy in such way as to relieve Banks."

An hour later Lincoln sent orders to General McDowell to suspend his movement on Richmond: "Gen. Frémont has been ordered by telegraph to move from Franklin on Harrisonburg, to relieve Gen. Banks and capture or destroy Jackson's and

Ewell's forces. You are instructed, laying aside for the present the movement on Richmond, to put twenty thousand men in motion at once for the Shenandoah, moving on the line, or in advance of the line of the Manassas Gap Railroad. Your object will be to capture the forces of Jackson and Ewell, either in cooperation with Gen. Frémont, or, in case want of supplies or if transportation interferes with his movement, it is believed that the force with which you move will be sufficient to accomplish the object alone. . . ."

Lincoln's overall plan, then, was for Banks to reform on or near the Potomac while Frémont moved towards Jackson's rear at Harrisonburg. McDowell would meanwhile advance west from Fredericksburg in case Stonewall moved east across the Blue Ridge. Either Frémont or McDowell alone supposedly had enough strength to defeat Jackson; if the two Union forces combined, the Valley could be cleared and Jackson eliminated. The plan looked very good on paper and could well have succeeded, except for the unpredictability of one man—Stonewall Jackson himself.

In his own eyes, Lincoln knew he was taking a risk by sending so many troops after Jackson. He was genuinely afraid that Jackson might escape from the Valley and descend on Washington, whose ragtag garrison might not have held back a determined enemy force. For that reason Lincoln ordered McDowell to send one of his brigades to Manassas and another to Washington; in addition, Stanton issued a call for militia from neighboring states. What concerned Lincoln most was McClellan's isolated position in far-off eastern Virginia. McClellan had been impossibly slow in mounting his campaign, and Lincoln's patience was now running thin. On 25 May Lincoln warned "Little Mac," "I think the time is near when you must either attack Richmond or give up the job and come to the defense of Washington."

Jackson on the Potomac

In view of his frustration over his inability to properly pursue the enemy after Winchester, it would be reasonable to expect that Jackson would have pushed his weary troops northward after Banks on 26 May, the day after his victory. Instead, Jackson, the master of the unexpected, issued an order to his men that the "Chief duty to-day, and that of the army, is to recognize devoutly the hand of a protecting Providence in the brilliant successes of the last three days (which have given us the results of a great victory without great losses), and to make the oblation of our thanks to God for his mercies to us and our country in heartfelt acts of religious worship. For this purpose the troops will remain in camp to-day, suspending, as far as possible, all military exercises; and the chaplains of regiments will hold divine service in their several charges at 4 o'clock P. M."

After a second full day of rest to recuperate from the vigors of the recent campaign, Stonewall was ready to resume action on 28 May. He was not then certain what his next objective should be. Frémont was too far away in the western mountains, while McDowell's force at Fredericksburg was probably too large to deal with. Banks' beat-up command seemed to be the best objective, even though it had retreated across the Potomac to Williamsport. Lee and Johnston had encouraged Stonewall to proceed north to the line of the Potomac so that he could threaten everyone from Pittsburgh to Baltimore. This certainly was not Jackson's immediate goal when he began marching on 28 May, though the same end result may have been on his mind.

Being a practical man, Jackson's first object was to see what Union troops remained on the southern side of the Potomac. On the morning of 28 May he sent the 2nd Virginia Cavalry to burn the railroad bridges at Martinsburg. He also sent Winder with four regiments of the Stonewall Brigade and two batteries to Harpers Ferry. A little bit south of Charlestown, Winder ran into a Federal reconnaissance forced composed of the *11th Pennsylvania Infantry*, the Unionist *1st Maryland Cavalry*, and two cannons.

The Federals formed a line to make a stand, but were soon scattered by several well placed shots from Capt. Joseph Carpenter's Virginia Battery. The Yankees retreated in haste to Bolivar Heights, on which was ensconced a strong but hastily assembled force under Brig. Gen. Rufus Saxton. When Saxton formed up his command in a line stretching from the Shenandoah to the Potomac it comprised 7000 men and 18 guns. Winder advanced as far as Halltown, but chose to withdraw to

Harpers Ferry changed hands numerous times during the war. Jackson occupied the town after the battle of Winchester, and captured 12,500 Federals there in September 1862.

Charlestown rather than confront Saxton's forces on Bolivar Heights.

When Jackson heard the size of the Union garrison at Harpers Ferry, he sent Ewell to support Winder. Ewell arrived at Charlestown at dark on the 28th. Jackson joined him there with the remainder of his own division on the 29th. From there he advanced his full force to face Saxton's line on Bolivar Heights. Except for sending the 2nd Virginia Infantry to Loudoun Heights on the southern side of the Shenandoah River across from Harpers Ferry, nothing much else happened on the 29th. Saxton, however, remained apprehensive, fearful that Jackson might be making a move in force against Loudoun Heights; he had also heard a rumor that Jackson was sending a division across the Potomac.

Jackson for once was stymied. Harpers Ferry looked like a tough nut to crack, and other developments showed that he had little time to work with. His scouts reported that McDowell's troops were moving towards Front Royal, while other dispatches reported that Frémont was moving north from Franklin and Banks had been reinforced and was coming south from Williamsport. If he stayed to attack Harpers Ferry or move against Banks, Jackson faced the distinct possibility of being trapped in the lower Valley within two or three days. The outcome of such an entrapment would not be pleasant for the Confederates, who would be outnumbered about 60,000 to 15,000. Jackson, tired as he was, knew that he had no choice but to withdraw in a hurry.

Jackson Eludes the Trap

On the rainy morning of 30 May Jackson sent his army on the road back to Winchester, and prepared to march or fight his way out of his predicament. He expressed his true intentions to his good friend, Congressman Alexander R. Boteler. He then sent Boteler to Richmond with a plea for reinforcements. Once he escaped Lincoln's trap, he was sure he could deal the Yankees a terrible blow if he received 20,000 or so reinforcements. Such a victory would relieve the siege of Richmond and "transfer his campaign from the banks of the Potomac to those of the Susquehanna."

As he journeyed through the rain from Harpers Ferry to Charlestown on the afternoon of the 30th, Jackson received the shocking news that Shields had captured Front Royal. Jackson had left Col. Z.T. Conner's 12th Georgia there, supported by two guns of Capt. William Rice's Virginia Battery, to guard the bridges and oversee the transfer south of the huge quantity of supplies that had been captured a few days earlier from "Commissary" Banks. Conner apparently was not keeping a very good lookout for the enemy. As a result he was totally surprised about noon on the 30th by Brig. Gen. James Shields with a small force of cavalry and a supporting infantry brigade. Conner's men fled to Winchester after burning the supplies that remained

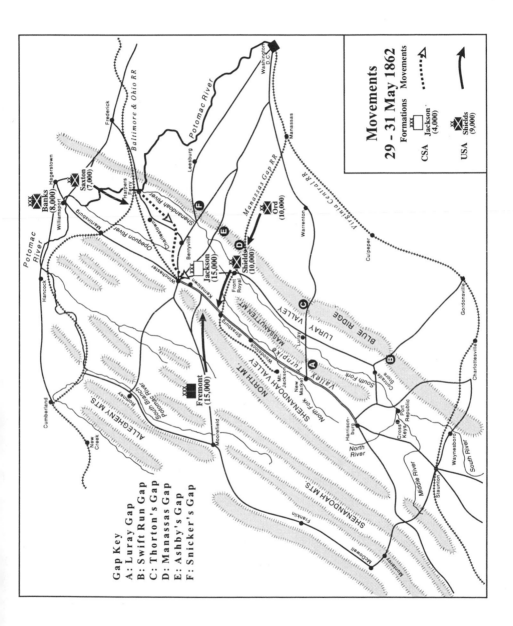

Gap Key
A: Luray Gap
B: Swift Run Gap
C: Thorton's Gap
D: Manassas Gap
E: Ashby's Gap
F: Snicker's Gap

Movements
29 - 31 May 1862
Formations   Movements
CSA   Jackson
(4,000)
USA   Shields
(9,000)

Frémont's Federals cross a pontoon bridge over the Shenandoah River. Heavy rains retarded his pursuit of Jackson's retreating army.

in town. At Winchester, the unfortunate colonel was placed under arrest by Jackson for putting up such a feeble defense.

Jackson realized that his predicament was worse than he had thought. Shields' force at Front Royal was only 18 miles from Jackson's army at Winchester. More importantly, it was only 12 miles from Strasburg, which was astride Jackson's line of retreat up the Valley Turnpike. If Shields occupied Strasburg in force, or, worse yet, met Frémont's army there, Jackson would be in real trouble. This seemed a distinct possibility, since Jackson was 40 miles from Strasburg, over three times as far from that critical junction as were Shields' men.

By nightfall of the 30th, Jackson had his whole force at Winchester except for the Stonewall Brigade, which had stayed at Bolivar Heights in order to keep Saxton in place by threatening an attack. Stonewall knew that he had to lead his exhausted troops south to Strasburg as quickly as possible in order to get there ahead of the Yankees, whom he probably would have to fight somewhere along the line. Full of anxiety, he had his troops

Harpers Ferry is located at the confluence of the Potomac and Shenan-doah Rivers. Its bridges were burned early in the war, and were replaced by military pontoon bridges.

up before dawn on 31 May. Fortunately the day would become bright and sunny; if it had been as rainy as the 30th, Jackson's men would not have been able to accomplish what had to be done. Stonewall arranged his line of march carefully. First, his mammoth wagon train—eight miles long and bulging with captured Yankee supplies—was sent south. Next came 2300 Union prisoners, guarded by the 21st Virginia. Finally came the weary infantry—Taliaferro's brigade, Campbell's brigade, Ewell's division. Closing this column, which stretched some 15 miles, were the remnants of his cavalry, which was kept busier

Brig. Gen. Charles S. Winder ably led the Stonewall Brigade during the height of the Valley Campaign. He was killed in action two months later at Cedar Mountain.

rounding up and aiding stragglers than it was fighting off the enemy.

The hardest march of all was faced by the Stonewall Brigade, which began the 31st opposite Bolivar Heights. Several delays hindered the prompt departure that the crisis demanded. It took a few hours for the 2nd Virginia to recross the Shenandoah River from Loudoun Heights. An unexpected delay occurred when Jed Hotchkiss, the army's mapmaker, whom Jackson had sent expressly for the purpose of guiding Winder, inexplicably got lost himself.

After a late start, Winder marched straight through to Winchester without stopping to eat. The men were already dropping from exhaustion when they arrived in the "Apple Blossom Capital," only to receive new orders to be at Strasburg by 0700 on 1 June. They did not understand why such a forced march had been ordered. Stonewall was capable of some pretty strange commands, but by now Winder had learned to obey Jackson without question. He pushed his men onward until his regiments were only skeletons; in so doing he lost more men as stragglers than he was able to keep with the colors. When he reached Newtown, Winder realized that he would have no one left in the ranks if he kept pushing on without respite to Strasburg, a goal that he could not reach on time anyway. Consequently, he let his men stop to sleep. His troops had done extraordinarily well to cover 30 miles in 14 hours; the 2nd Virginia had marched 35 from its advanced position.

Miraculously, Jackson had reached Strasburg ahead of the converging Union columns. His early forced march on 31 May showed a determination both Shields and Frémont lacked. Neither Yankee commander had the drive of Stonewall, and both feared running head on into Jackson's force, which outnumbered each individual Union column. As Jackson's forces shuffled through Strasburg, the head of Frémont's column was only five miles to the west, and Shields was closer than that on the east. Jackson had come within a few hours of having to fight his way through at Strasburg, or even of being bottled up in the lower Valley.

Indeed, Jackson would have lost his race if Frémont or Shields had been more aggressive. Two other factors also aided Jackson's cause, though he was not aware of them at the time. Shields was supposed to have been supported by Brig. Gen. Edward O.C. Ord's division, coming up from the Rappahannock. Ord, however, had been directed to take part of his journey west by canal boat. This slowed him down so much that he was almost a full day's march behind Shields. Shields, with only 10,000 men, slowed his pace, because he was reluctant to face Jackson's 17,000 without Ord's aid. Meanwhile, Frémont heard that the passes between Franklin and New Market were still blocked by the trees and boulders Jed Hotchkiss and his men had put there during the McDowell campaign. He decided to march via Moorefield, to Strasburg rather than Harrisonburg, as ordered. This was a longer route through the mountains, and even then he did not speed up his pace any. As a result, neither Frémont nor Shields arrived at Strasburg in time to snap shut Lincoln's trap.

Though by superhuman effort Jackson's men had reached Strasburg first, they were still not yet out of danger. On 1 June Jackson sent Ewell's division west to support Ashby, who was

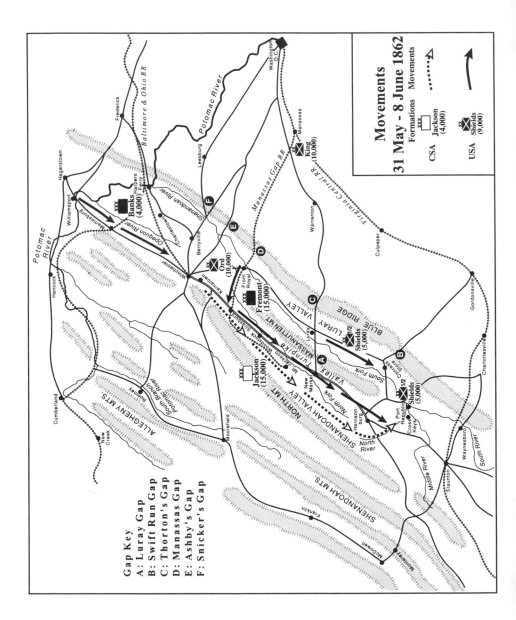

beginning to have difficulty keeping Frémont back. Ewell met Col. Gustav P. Cluseret's *Advance Brigade* (a special mixed command of infantry, cavalry, and artillery) about three miles west of Strasburg, and brought the Yankee column to a halt. The two sides at first skirmished heavily, then backed off. Frémont was reluctant to engage Jackson's whole force before his entire command was up, so he disengaged and advanced no farther that day. To the east, Shields was experiencing indecision also. Ord's division began arriving in driblets, but not in chunks large enough to encourage Shields to strike at Jackson aggressively. Shields was also confused about where Frémont's command was—he heard the sound of the skirmish between Frémont and Ewell coming from the northwest of Strasburg, not from the southwest, as he expected according to Lincoln's orders to Frémont. For a while Shields directed his column towards Winchester in an attempt to catch Jackson, but this soon proved to be wasted effort. Upon realizing his mistake, General McDowell, who was then accompanying Shields, sent Shields south to try to catch up with Jackson, who by now had a half day head start.

Stonewall was frankly astonished, but thankful, that Shields did not press him harder. All the while that Shields' men were marching in circles east of Front Royal, Winder was pushing his men south as hard as he could. When he heard the guns of Ewell's skirmish with Frémont, he was sure that the turnpike would be blocked at Middletown. As he approached that village, Winder formed a heavy skirmish line and prepared for the worst. Much to his surprise, the only troops he ran into at Middletown were Ashby and his cavalry. As Winder rode up to confer with Ashby, the cavalry leader cracked, "General, I never was so relieved in my life. I thought you would be cut off and had made up my mind to join you and advise you to make your escape over the mountains to Gordonsville."

After passing Middletown, Winder reached Strasburg at noon. Soon afterwards Jackson withdrew Ewell's detachment that had been holding off Frémont, and the whole Valley army headed for Harrisonburg. That night most of the army encamped exhausted but relieved at Woodstock. The cavalry, forming the rear guard, spent the night four miles south of

Woodstock. Everyone down to the lowest private was well aware of the scrape they had just passed through. Jackson's foot cavalry had simply outmarched the Yankees, covering 50 to 60 miles in three days while Frémont and Shields advanced less than half that distance.

As soon as Stonewall's rear guard left Strasburg, Cluseret's *Advance Brigade* seized the town. Some of the Union cavalry continued on until they struck Jackson's cavalry rear guard about four miles to the south. In the darkness, the Yankees managed to bypass the pickets of the 6th Virginia Cavalry and strike the main Confederate camp, but they were soon repulsed and driven off.

Frémont himself did not enter Strasburg with most of his troops until early on 1 June. As he passed through the town, he met the advance elements of Shields' cavalry under Brig. Gen. George D. Bayard. As the forces of Frémont and Shields met, the Union trap snapped shut—24 hours too late to catch Stonewall Jackson.

Jackson Falls Back

As Jackson continued south along the Valley Turnpike, he was uncertain what his next step should be. He had given the Yankees the slip, but he was still in grave danger. If Shields and Frémont had united their forces at Strasburg and were following him up the Valley, there was no way he could turn to offer battle at the moment; the best he could do would be to draw them farther south in hope of catching them in an error or pouncing on a detachment. The least he could do in such a situation would be to detain as many of the enemy as possible away from the main battle at Richmond.

Another scenario was much less attractive to Jackson. Stonewall was concerned that most of the enemy contact he had been having for the past few days was with Frémont's command; Shields had not been very aggressive and now had dropped out of sight. Jackson had to consider that Shields might be marching up the Luray Valley under cover of the Massanutten Mountains with the goal of getting into Jackson's rear by way of the New Market Gap. To forestall this possibility, Jackson sent a cavalry force to burn the only two bridges over the South Fork of the Shenandoah near Luray. When this mission was accomplished, Jackson could rest more easily, confident that Shields would be unable to reach the New Market Gap. If Shields wished to get behind Jackson now, he would have to find a new ford across the river, or proceed 20 miles south of Luray to cross the Shenandoah at Conrad's Store and then circle the south end of the Massanutten range at Cross Keys and Harrisonburg. Since Jackson would have the use of the macadamized Valley Turnpike going south and Shields, if he were heading south, would be using inferior country roads, Jackson was likely to reach Harrisonburg ahead of the Yankees.

Yet, Jackson could take nothing for granted. If there was any chance that the Yankees might get into his rear, he had to deal with it. Though his men were dog tired, he had them march all night on 1 June in order to put some distance between him and the enemy. The next day he proceeded to Mount Jackson, and on the 3rd he retired to New Market. After burning the Rude's Hill bridge over the North Fork of the Shenandoah, the army limped on. The destruction of this key span brought Jackson's men only temporary respite from their pursuers. Unknown to Jackson, Frémont had pontoon equipment with him. With unusual alacrity, Frémont built a new bridge and was ready to pursue Stonewall after only a slight delay.

Frémont had just completed his pontoon bridge when the skies opened up in a terrible rainstorm. The campaign had already been afflicted by frequent rains that dampened the men's spirits and slowed down their movement. Now the bad weather was beginning to affect strategy. The rapidly rising North Fork of the Shenandoah threatened to wash out Frémont's newly built pontoon bridge; logs and other drift carried by the swift current smashed into the boats supporting it. To save the bridge from being completely destroyed, Frémont ordered the stanchion ropes to be cut at their southern end. The bridge was then swung over to the north shore, though only after the loss of much timber and planking. That night the storm waters resided. Though the troops worked hard, the bridge was not reassembled and ready for use until 1000 the next morning.

This single rainstorm cost 28 hours in Frémont's pursuit of Jackson.

Besides slowing down Frémont, the heavy rains made Jackson alter his course. He had entertained thoughts of retiring towards Staunton, but to get there he would have to cross the swollen North River, which was at its highest level in 20 years. His only other reasonable course, short of abandoning the Shenandoah, was to march southwest of Harrisonburg to Port Republic, which had a sturdy bridge over the North River that had so far survived the floods. Control of this key bridge would give him the freedom to move against either Frémont or Shields; destruction of the bridge would continue to keep his two opponents apart. However, Stonewall was aware that he had run out of running room and now had to fight or abandon the Valley completely. In addition, the enemy would be able to cross the North River as soon as its flood waters subsided.

As Jackson moved to Port Republic, he prepared his army for action. He sent Jed Hotchkiss to establish a signal station on the southern end of the Massanutten range in order to keep an eye on Shields' movements. A cavalry force was also sent to burn the bridge over the South Fork of the Shenandoah at Conrad's Store. Shields had sent a small cavalry force to guard the bridge, but the Confederate raiders outfoxed them and accomplished their mission. The destruction of this bridge guaranteed that Shields would have to remain east of the South Fork in the Luray Valley. The next crossing point over the river was 13 miles southeast of Conrad's Store at Port Republic—which was Jackson's destination.

Jackson also took the precaution of stripping down his army for battle. He had already sent his prisoners and most of his wagons from Winchester over the mountains to Waynesboro. On 4 June, as soon as the flood waters on the North River subsided somewhat, Jackson determined to send his sick and wounded across the muddy river to safety in Staunton. His pioneers worked all morning on the 5th to create a ferry. The army's sick and their ambulances were then transported across the North River despite considerable danger.

Jackson now led his army southeast from Harrisonburg. He then left the Valley Pike and exchanged its familiar roadway for

The **Pennsylvania Bucktails** *fight Ashby's cavalry during the sharp skirmish at Harrisonburg on 6 June.*

less sturdy local roads. It was not long before his supply and ammunition wagons were mired in the mud. It was another crisis of the campaign. The key town of Port Republic had to be reached before Shields arrived there, and Frémont was breathing hard down Jackson's back. The army had lost hundreds of stragglers and could now field less than 12,000 men; some regiments were being led by captains, and everyone was totally exhausted.

The march had been particularly difficult for the Confederate rear guard, which was being pressed hard by the Yankees. On 1 June the 2nd Virginia Cavalry had been surprised and routed by Union cavalry, and in their flight they disorganized much of

Taylor's brigade. The next morning more confusion arose when Steuart's cavalry relieved Taylor's infantry as rear guard. Steuart mishandled the positioning of his men, and once again the Yankees took advantage of the situation to temporarily rout the Confederate cavalry. The moment was saved only when Ashby saw the confusion and quickly gathered about 50 infantry stragglers into a makeshift line. This improvised force delayed the Union cavalry long enough for Col. John M. Patton—temporarily commanding Campbell's brigade—to send back an infantry regiment to set the Yankees flying. Because of Steuart's ineptitude on this occasion, Ewell requested that the erstwhile cavalry commander be returned to an infantry command. Jackson acquiesced, and transferred Steuart to command of Scott's brigade in Ewell's division. The 2nd and 6th Virginia Cavalry Regiments were then transferred to Ashby's command. Ashby had been promoted to brigadier general on 23 March, and now finally had a real brigade of three regiments.

Contact between Jackson and Frémont—which had been lost when Frémont had to repair his bridge over the North Ford—was resumed about noon on 6 June, shortly after Jackson abandoned Harrisonburg. Turner Ashby, who was commanding Jackson's rear guard as usual, allowed the Yankees to move into Harrisonburg unopposed while he took up a position two miles south of the town. About an hour later the Union advance caught up to Ashby's lines. One of the more exciting cavalry engagements of the war ensued.

Cavalry Clash

The Union troopers that attacked Ashby just south of Harrisonburg on the afternoon of 6 June 1862 were commanded by Sir Percy Wyndham, an English soldier of fortune who was then commanding the *1st New Jersey Cavalry* of Bayard's brigade. Wyndham, one of the most competent and aggressive Union cavalry commanders at that stage of the war, that day was leading Frémont's advance guard, about 800 men in the *1st New Jersey*, *1st Pennsylvania*, *4th New York*, and *1st Connecticut Cavalry Regiments*. Wyndham's advance was described by a Union officer who was present, "About half-past one o'clock Col.

Brig. Gen. Turner Ashby was the dynamic but undisciplined leader of Jackson's cavalry. His boldness caused his death at Harrisonburg on 6 June 1862.

Wyndham made his move, and went through the long main street of the town at a rapid trot. Arriving on the other side, the column turned to the left and advanced through two or three fields to the summit of a hill overlooking an open valley, from which rose another hill beyond, covered with woods. The cavalry were halted, and skirmishers sent ahead and on the flanks. They were gone some time, and returned with no satisfactory report. Nevertheless, Col. Wyndham, though he had reached the point beyond which he was ordered not to push his reconnaissance, decided to advance. With full knowledge that the enemy was somewhere in front of him, whom he might have to charge at any moment, he nevertheless hurried on his tired horses, advancing for more than two miles at an unbroken trot. The enemy's cavalry were suddenly discovered in front, drawn up, as usual, across the road, and extending into the woods on either side."

Ashby's front line at the moment Wyndham attacked consisted of the 6th Virginia Cavalry; he was holding his other two regiments in reserve to allow his men to rest and the horses to graze. Always fond of a good fight, Ashby shouted for his men to form up as soon as he saw Wyndham's attack. In no time at all he was leading a mad charge against the Yankees.

Attack of the 1st Maryland (CSA) at Harrisonburg on 6 June 1862, during which Brig. Gen. Turner Ashby was killed.

Our Union source continues: "It was impossible to determine their force, and there was no support within three or four miles. But Col. Wyndham determined to attack, and, without any attempt to discover by skirmishing the strength or position of the enemy, or whether any infantry were opposed to him, ordered a charge, and rashly led his own regiment, the First New Jersey cavalry straight up the hill. On the left there was nothing but woods. On the right, for some distance before the rebel line was reached, was a field of wheat. In this field was concealed a strong body, not less than a regiment, of rebel infantry [actually dismounted cavalry]. They were not completely screened from view by the tall grain, but were visible at least to the officers and men of the second squadron. Utterly unsuspicious of such a force on his flank, Col. Wyndham charged with speed up the hill. When the first squadron was fairly within the line of flanking fire the rebels poured in a volley, which, coming so close at hand and on the flank, threw the whole squadron into confusion, Col. Wyndham's horse was shot from under him, and he was taken prisoner. . . . All the officers bravely but vainly endeavored to rally their men, and

President Lincoln's grand plan to trap Jackson in the lower Valley failed because of excess caution shown by his commanders in the field. He learned his lesson and afterwards did not intervene as actively in the direction of military campaigns.

after one or two feeble efforts to hold their ground the first battalion was driven down the hill. Capt. Janeway, Company L, who was leading the second squadron, perceiving as he advanced up the hill that the wheat-field covered a force of infantry, as soon as the first squadron was thrown into disorder by the unexpected fire on the flank, endeavored to lead his men through the woods on the left of the road, in order to shelter them from the infantry fire and to flank the cavalry on the hill. This movement was skillfully planned, but before it could be wholly executed part of the squadron was thrown into confusion by the retreat of the advance, which came down the hill in disorderly flight, and nothing was left to do but to retire."

Ashby's mad charge certainly had been a complete success. At the loss of only one man wounded, he caused 36 enemy combat casualties and captured Colonel Wyndham along with 63 members of his command. Wyndham was boiling mad to be led captive by the damned rebels he had vowed to catch himself. Ashby, meanwhile, had his fighting blood up. Ewell had sent some infantry support in the form of the 1st Maryland and 58th Virginia, and Ashby quickly devised a strategem to impose still more embarrassment on the enemy.

Ashby's plan was to lay an ambush with the two infantry regiments Ewell had sent, and use his own cavalry as the bait. As he marched his men into a woods to deploy them, he was totally unaware that the Yankee advance guard had been even more heavily reinforced than his own command. Right after Wyndham was engaged, General Bayard himself rushed forward with the *60th Ohio* and *8th West Virginia* (both under Colonel Cluseret) and four companies of the *Bucktail Rifles* (the *13th Pennsylvania Reserves*), one of the crack sharpshooter units in the Union army.

Ashby's overconfidence and sloppy manner of field command now caught up with him. He had no skirmishers out as he led the 58th Virginia into position, and walked into a Union ambush himself. The *Bucktail Rifles* opened fire, and the startled 58th Virginia wavered and broke. The valiant Ashby rushed forward to rally his line and organize a charge. His horse was shot dead, but he bounded up shouting, "Charge, men! For God's sake, charge!" His courage rallied the 58th while the 1st Maryland struck the Yankees on the flanks and Col. Thomas T. Munford's 2nd Virginia Cavalry charged them head on. The Union advance was blunted, and the *Bucktails* were soon driven back streaming towards Harrisonburg. In 15 minutes of sharp fighting, the *Bucktails* lost 55 men, in addition to their commander, Col. Thomas L. Kane, who was captured. Rebel losses were slightly heavier, 17 killed, 50 wounded and 3 missing.

As the smoke cleared, Ashby was nowhere to be seen. He was finally found as the casualties on the field were being cleaned up. He had been shot dead soon after his horse went down. His men could hardly believe it. Ashby had always been in the thick of the fight and had had several close calls, but he seemed to lead a charmed life. Now he was gone. And his men began to doubt their own invincibility. His body, wrapped in a Confederate flag, was sent to Port Republic. All of Virginia mourned him, as a great hero fallen in battle.

Turner Ashby, Valley Cavalier

Turner Ashby (1828–1862), leader of the Valley army's cavalry, was an even more colorful figure than Stonewall Jackson. A man of great skill, particularly at leading cavalry raids, he also had more than his share of faults, especially in the administrative area. Ashby's bravery and impetuosity made him the hero of his men, and his early death at the height of the Valley Campaign made him Virginia's first great martyr to the Southern cause.

Ashby came from a long line of Virginia country gentlemen. His great-great-grandfather Capt. Thomas Ashby, had settled in Fauquier County soon after 1700. Thomas' oldest son, John, was reportedly the first white man to drive a wagon into the Shenandoah Valley; Ashby's Gap in the Blue Ridge Mountains was named after him. John settled on the banks of the Shenandoah at Ashby's Ferry, later called Berry's Ferry, and began acquiring the land holdings that formed the basis of the family's fortune. John was also one of the first explorers of Kentucky in the days of Daniel Boone.

Of all his ancestors, Turner was thought to resemble his great-grandfather John the most in actions and temperament. From his other forbears he inherited the love for horsemanship and action that characterized so many of the young men who grew up in the Piedmont, as well as a love for military service. John served with Braddock and Washington in 1754; John II was a captain in the Revolution; and Turner's father, also named Turner

Ashby, was a colonel in the War of 1812.

Turner Ashby, Sr., died in 1834 when his son was only 6. His widow, Elizabeth, was a determined and loving woman who would have nothing but the best for her six children. Turner was educated by private tutors and then attended a neighborhood school. He did not receive advanced formal education because this was not the custom for young gentlemen of his station and locale; instead, he lived an enviable life of riding, hunting, and helping to manage the family estate at Rose Hill. Unfortunately, running the farm proved to be too much financially, and Mrs. Ashby was forced to sell Rose Hill in 1853. Turner then bought his own farm nearby, which he named Wolfe's Crag, so called because of its situation on a high hill. He was thought to be quite handsome and reportedly broke the hearts of many belles, but he never married. Turner held several local political offices, and was one of the social leaders of his county.

In 1855–1856 Ashby found his true calling, the organization of a cavalry company to help police the workers who were constructing the Manassas Gap Railroad. He kept his company together and even expanded it. It was as if he foresaw the coming of the war, and wanted to be ready for it as soon as it broke out. When John Brown raided Harpers Ferry in October 1859, Ashby's cavalry was one of the first military units on the scene. Not wishing to miss any of the action, Ashby and his men stayed around until Brown was tried and hanged on 2 December.

When the Civil War began, Captain Ashby and his men immediately offered their services to the Confederacy. They were assigned to the command of Col. Thomas Jackson at Harpers Ferry, and were given the task of picketing the Potomac between Harpers Ferry and Point of Rocks. Here Ashby carried out his duties so well that in late April his men were designated Company A of the 7th Virginia Cavalry, and Turner was appointed the regiment's lieutenant colonel, his brother Richard succeeding him as commander of Company A. The two brothers were very close, and when Richard was killed in a skirmish on 26 June, Turner became even more daring and determined in his dealings with the enemy.

It was not long before the commander of the 7th Virginia Cavalry, Col. Angus McDonald, took leave from the army; the rigors of active campaigning were too much for a man in his 60s. This left the regiment to Ashby. In this capacity he helped Jeb Stuart screen Patterson's Union army while Joe Johnston's command hurried from the Valley to join Beauregard at Manassas and defeat McDowell's Union army at First Bull Run on 21 July. After their screening mission, Ashby and his men rode hard to reach Bull Run, but they arrived after the battle was over.

Ashby led his men back to the Valley, where they became part of Jackson's Valley army. They were sent on numerous scouting expeditions, and Ashby's bravery became well known to all. At one point he dressed as an old horse doctor and, mounted on an old nag, rode as far north as Pennsylvania to spy on the enemy. On 16 December 1861 he was near the Potomac with Captain Poague's battery. When the party was shelled by enemy artillery, all the gunners ran off leaving Ashby alone as he paced back and forth under fire. Poague immediately decided that Ashby was the bravest man he ever saw.

Ashby's fearlessness continued right to the end; he in fact appears to have cultivated it in order to enhance his reputation. As commander of the army's rear guard during the retreat from Winchester on 12 March 1862 Ashby was the last man to leave town. He deliberately waited until the incoming Yankees came into sight, and then calmly began riding out of town. Supposedly he ran into two enemy cavalrymen on the outskirts of town, killing one and taking the other prisoner. Ashby once said he never feared confronting the enemy, while on scout or skirmish. He felt that Yankee marksmanship was so bad that they never hit what they aimed at. It was the stray bullets he really feared, because they struck randomly and without warning.

Ashby's bravery brought numerous other cavaliers of kindred spirit to join him. At one point in April his regiment grew to more than 20 companies, over twice the usual allotment of 10. This number was far too many for any one commander to handle, especially Ashby. Ashby's one major weakness was administration and the enforcement of discipline. Wartime heroics, to him and his associates, came from raiding the enemy, not from filling in papers or from drilling. This lack of concern for military proprieties at times cost Ashby and his command dearly. On 16 April one of his companies was encamped near Columbia Furnace with no pickets posted; they were all captured by the enemy. The next day Ashby himself was unable to see to the burning of a key bridge over the North Fork of the Shenandoah at Rude's Hill. He was almost felled by enemy fire, and escaped on a mortally wounded horse. Individual heroism could only accomplish so much, and the key bridge was not burned as ordered.

Jackson's response to this situation was typical. He had for some time been annoyed at the lack of discipline in Ashby's command. In view of Ashby's failures in the field, on 24 April Jackson assigned his cavalry to Brig. Gen. W. B. Taliaferro. Ashby was given command of the "advance or rear guard," but had been effectively stripped of his command. The furious Ashby told a staff officer that he would have challenged Jackson to a duel if the two officers had been of the same rank. What Ashby did do was to tender his resignation. After an unsatisfactory meeting with Jackson, Ashby stormed off threatening to take his command out of Jackson's army. Jackson finally had to back down, one of the few times he did so, and he reinstated Ashby in command of his cavalry. Jackson knew that he needed Ashby's services, even if they were unorthodox. Stonewall nonetheless never did fully appreciate Ashby- for example, he never congratulated the cavalryman on his promotion to colonel in October 1861 or when he was promoted to brigadier general on 23 May 1862.

Ashby and his men fought well at Kernstown, a battle that Ashby helped initiate. It was he who scouted the situation and convinced Jackson that most of the Yankees had left Winchester-a mistaken impression that brought on the loss of the battle. Ashby's men successfully screened the Confederate left while Jackson kept feeding most of his men into the unsuccessful fight on the right. Ashby then led the army's rear guard and was among the last to leave the field.

Ashby did not participate in the McDowell operation because he was sick. His presence was sorely missed at McDowell and in the Valley, where his unruly men took to racing and carousing.

Ashby's strengths and weaknesses continued to be evident at Front Royal and Winchester. In the attack on Front Royal he did a marvelous job helping to isolate Kenly's Union garrison from Winchester. But he and his men were not immediately at hand when Jackson sorely needed them to pursue Banks' retreating army after the victory at Winchester. It is still not clear where Ashby was at that critical moment, or what he was doing. It is probable that many of his men had dispersed to plunder captured Union supplies, a sorry and unsatisfactory state of affairs.

Ashby and his men performed much better during the hurried retreat from Harpers Ferry to Winchester and beyond at the end of May. They formed the rear guard and skirmished daily with the enemy, whose forces were now much more aggressive and energetic under Col. George Bayard. Ashby's love for action is evidenced by the many times he was nearly wounded or had horses shot from under him. His luck finally ran out near Harrisonburg on 6 June 1862. Ashby was buried in Charlottesville, since his home in Fauquier County was then behind enemy lines. Later his body was removed to Lexington and buried in the cemetery there, near his old commander, Stonewall.

Ashby's death came as a severe blow to the Confederates, who had come to regard him as invincible. Even Jackson was affected, noting that "as a partisan officer I never knew his superior; his daring was proverbial; his powers of endurance almost incredible, his tone of character heroic; and his sagacity almost intuitive in divining the purposes and movements of the enemy." By his premature death Ashby became a larger than life hero, the image of the pure cavalier who fearlessly laid down his life for his country. He accomplished about all that could be done by bravery alone, and in the end perished by that very bravery, leading a charge against the enemy. A warrior such as he could ask for no better death.

Jackson and Washington D.C.

There is no doubt that Jackson's successes, particularly his defeat of Banks at Winchester on 25 May 1862, had deep effects on the Union high command in Washington. Lincoln's deliberate decision to send most of McDowell's command to help trap Jackson in the Valley seriously affected McClellan's drive on Richmond. McClellan had been anticipating McDowell's arrival to put pressure on the north side of Richmond, and he was still waiting in late June when Lee began the Seven Days' Battles. McDowell's rerouting changed the whole nature of the confrontation at Richmond, particularly on the Confederate side. Joe Johnston, and then Lee, feared the results of McDowell's arrival, and Johnston even went so far as to plan a preemptive strike against McClellan on 28 or 29 May rather than wait for McDowell to approach. Johnston called his attack off when most of McDowell's command was directed to the Valley.

However, did Jackson ever actually plan a direct attack on Washington? Early historians of the war, including the noted English scholar J.F.C. Fuller, asserted that Jackson's entire campaign was expressly designed to threaten Washington. This interpretation flaunts the actual events of the campaign. It also grossly overestimates Jackson's potential. With only 3500 men at his disposal at the time of Kernstown, he would have been unable to get near Washington. Even at the height of his strength, he only had 17,000 men—a force far from sufficient to attack Washington, which was then guarded by some 30,000 men, not to mention the 60,000 or more in Banks' and McDowell's commands that would have had to be dealt with. Jubal Early on 11-12 July 1864 managed to attack Washington with only 14,000 men. But at that time Washington had only a small covering force outside its defenses, a force that Early easily defeated at Winchester and Monocacy. It should also be noted that Early had no intention of actually taking Washington; he just wanted to create a big scare in the Lincoln Administration.

The most definitive statement of Jackson's intentions in regard to Washington comes from Jackson's utter silence on the subject. Twice he suggested to authorities in Richmond that, if reinforced, he would see that the war was carried into Pennsylvania. At no point did he mention attacking Washington. This prospect was actually only suggested once, in a letter written by Joe Johnston on 27 May 1862.

Nor did Lincoln and Stanton seem particularly concerned that Jackson might attack Washington. Several times Lincoln allowed Washington's garrison to be weakened to reinforce McClellan, McDowell, or Banks. Their only real concern for Washington's safety arose right after Banks' defeat at Winchester on 25 May. In spite of their concern, however, Lincoln and Stanton continued sending new volunteer troops to Banks as they arrived in the capital. They did take the unusual step of calling out nearby state militias to help defend Washington, but this measure was not carried through and served only to elicit comments in the Northern press about confusion the militia would cause in the capital.

The Geography of the Valley

In order to appreciate the military campaign of 1862 it is absolutely necessary to understand the geography of the Shenandoah Valley. The Valley lies on what is now the western edge of Virginia, between the Piedmont uplands on the east and the Allegheny Mountains on the west. Drained almost exclusively by the Shenandoah River and its tributaries, the Valley runs southwest from the Potomac River 150 miles to the headlands of the James River. The Valley is bounded directly by the Blue Ridge Mountains on the east and the North Mountains on the west, and varies in width from 15 miles at its northern extremity to 30 at its southern end.

In practical terms, the Valley can be divided into three sections of approximately equal size. The lower Valley runs for about 35 miles from the Potomac River to the Massanutten Mountains, about which more will be said shortly. Its major feature is the Shenandoah River, which is formed a few miles west of Front Royal by the confluence of the North Fork and the South Fork. It flows northeast along the eastern edge of the Valley to Harpers Ferry, where it joins the Potomac. The lower Valley's other river, the Opequon, is much less of a military obstacle, running on the Valley's western side from near Winchester, to join the Potomac near Martinsburg.

During the Civil War the lower Valley was relatively accessible from all directions except the southwest. On its northeast side, the Potomac River was crossed by fords at Falling Waters and Shepherdstown, and by a railroad brigade at Harpers Ferry. To the southeast, the Blue Ridge Mountains are crossed by several gaps. From north to south the most important of these are Snicker's, Ashby's, Manassas, and Chester; the North Mountains were also crossed by several gaps. Only on the southwest is there limited access to the lower Valley, for there the North Fork of the Shenandoah runs across the northern base of the Massanuttens.

This geography made three cities in the lower Valley militarily important. Harpers Ferry held a critical position astride the Baltimore and Ohio Railroad and the Chesapeake and Ohio Canal, both of which were major supply links between Washington, D. C., and the west; Harpers Ferry was also the terminus for a railroad spur that extended southwest to Winchester, the lower Valley's oldest town, founded in 1743. For all its military importance, Harpers Ferry was a difficult post to defend, being dominated on the southeast by Loudoun Heights and on the southwest by Bolivar Heights. The second key town in the lower Valley was Front Royal, which controlled the important bridges over the North and South Forks of the Shenandoah. It also controlled the Manassas Gap Railroad, which ran from the middle Valley through Manassas Gap to Manassas Junction, where it linked up with

Virginia's main railroad system. The third key town in the lower Valley was Strasburg, near the North Fork, at the western corner of the lower Valley. Strasburg was situated on the Manassas Gap Railroad, near the bridge which carried the railroad over the North Fork of the Shenandoah.

The middle Valley stretches southwest for about 35 miles from the confluence of the North and South Forks at Front Royal to Harrisonburg. This section of the Valley is unique because it is divided in its entirety by the Massanutten Mountains, which rise up suddenly between Strasburg and Front Royal and stretches continuously southwest until it abruptly ends near Harrisonburg. The Massanuttens divide the Valley into two sections. The smaller or eastern portion is called the Luray Valley, after its principal town; the Luray Valley is drained by the South Fork and has two principal outlets to the east, Fishers Gap at nearly its midpoint and Swift Run Gap, at its southern end. The larger or western portion of the middle Valley retains the name Shenandoah Valley. It is drained by the North Fork, and is also accessible from the west through several gaps in the North Mountains.

Militarily, the Shenandoah section of the middle Valley was much more important than the Luray Valley. The Luray Valley was less prosperous and less populated, and had a less well developed road system. The Shenandoah Valley contained a modern macadamized road, the Valley Turnpike, running its entire length, as well as a spur of the Manassas Gap Railroad, which ran from Strasburg, at the head of the middle Valley, halfway down the section's length to Mount Jackson, which had that name long before Stonewall Jackson became famous. By far the most important town in the middle Valley was New Market, located between the North Fork and the only pass through the Massanutten; control of the New Market Pass gave great maneuverability and offered valuable strategic options for advancing up either the Luray Valley or the Shenandoah Valley. Other key towns in the middle Valley were Strasburg, at the northern entrance to the sector; Front Royal, at the northern end of the Luray Valley; and Harrisonburg, at the southern end of the Shenandoah Valley segment. Possession of these three towns gave control of the entire middle Valley, as well as access to the lower and upper valleys.

The third, or upper section, of the Valley extended over 60 miles from the southwestern tip of the Massanuttens to the headwaters of the James River. This section was broader and more fertile than the middle or lower sections, and contained larger towns: Staunton, astride the important Virginia Central Railroad that ran from Charlottesville west to Tennessee, and Lexington, the home of Washington College and V.M.I. The upper Valley was readily accessible at its southwest edge and through several passes in the Blue Ridge Mountains on its southeastern edge. Its western edge was bounded by the Allegheny Mountains, and access from the north was restricted by the fords over the North River, which ran across most of the upper Valley from west to east, to meet the South River at Port Republic, there form-

ing the South Fork of the Shenandoah. The most militarily important towns of the upper Valley during Jackson's campaign were Harrisonburg, astride the Valley Turnpike at the northern entrance of the upper Valley, and Port Republic, which controlled east-west traffic with its bridges over the North and South Rivers. The South Fork of the Shenandoah River north of Port Republic had only three bridges in the Luray Valley, one at Conrad's Store and two near the New Market Gap.

The Shenandoah Valley was, and still is, one of the most beautiful spots in America. It was also known for its agriculture—the Valley's underlying limestone produces rich harvests and luxuriant grasses—and light industry. As a result, the Valley was known as the "Granary of the Confederacy," and produced far more food than it needed for its own use. It was also second only to Kentucky in production of horses and mules. Industrially, the Valley was the home of Cyrus McCormick's reaper, invented in 1831 and produced in Harrisonburg. The Valley boasted numerous iron forges, wool factories, flour mills, and lumber mills.

The link that tied the whole Valley together was the Valley Turnpike, which ran for 80 miles from Winchester to Staunton. It was opened in 1840, and was a wonder for its deliberate attempt to be as straight as possible. The road was "macadamized" in the then modern fashion, being constructed of gravel layers set on a cement bed, with limestone shoulders. The pike offered speedy travel up and down the Valley, especially when rains turned all the other roads to mud.

CHAPTER VII

Twin Battles

7–12 June 1862

*J*ackson rested his men most of 6 June as the wagons rolled to safety via Port Republic. He tried to tempt Frémont to attack, but the Yankee was too cautious. That evening he gave up, and marched his own division to Port Republic, leaving Ewell behind to face Frémont. As far as he was concerned, his campaign was just about over. That evening he wrote to Richmond, "My present position is such that if Shields forms a junction with Frémont by moving west he will have to do so by marching within about two miles of my advanced brigade or else he must return to New Market. Should my command be required at Richmond I can be at Mechum's River Depot, on the Central Railroad, the second day's march, and part of the command can reach there the first day, as the distance is 25 miles. At present I do not see that I can do much more than rest my command and devote its time to drilling. My advanced brigade is about seven miles this side of Harrisonburg. If Shields crosses the Blue Ridge shall my entire command, or any part of it, move correspondingly?"

Jackson's communique is important for showing that he had no immediate offensive planned. He was simply going to sit where he was in order to prevent Frémont and Shields from joining forces, and then await orders from Richmond.

In order to fully understand what happened next, we must review the important geography of the Port Republic area. The

town itself was of no consequence, being only about 50 buildings with no major industry. What was important about the
town was its location on a peninsula at the confluence of the
North River (flowing from the west) and the South River
(flowing from the south), which came together at the eastern
edge of the town to form the South Fork of the Shenandoah
River. A short distance upstream from this confluence was a
bridge over the North River. This bridge was the only crossing
place for many miles upstream; the nearest crossing downstream from this bridge was 13 miles northeast at Conrad's
Store, a bridge already destroyed at Jackson's orders. The South
River was much less of an obstacle than the North River or the
South Fork. It was crossable at two fords near the town, and at
other points upstream.

Jackson's immediate goal, was to keep control of—or destroy—the Port Republic bridge in order to keep Frémont and
Shields from uniting. For the moment Stonewall chose to leave
the bridge intact because its survival offered attractive possibilities for maneuver. If pressed too closely, he could simply cross
the bridge, burn it, and proceed on his way. For the moment,
then, he left Ewell's division to face Frémont, and posted his
own division within supporting distance of Ewell on the north
bank of the South Fork. There, Jackson occupied a line of bluffs
that dominated the approach on the other side of the river to
Port Republic. Since there was as yet no sign of Frémont,
Jackson posted only a small guard in Port Republic itself. He
was still hoping to entice Frémont into attacking Ewell; he
would then lead his own division in a counterattack that would
defeat the Federals.

On Saturday evening, 7 June 1862, Jackson held his full
attention on Frémont's force. He placed his headquarters on the
southwestern edge of Port Republic at the estate of Dr. George
Kemper. To the south were parked most of the army's wagons.
There was no garrison in the town except the six guns of Capt.
James Carrington's newly raised battery. Two cavalry companies that had been posted in town were sent east to keep an eye
on Shields.

Combat at Port Republic

The scene at Port Republic was peaceful and serene on the morning of 8 June. About 0800 Jackson was conversing with several members of his staff on Dr. Kemper's veranda when suddenly, out of the blue, a detachment of Union cavalry came dashing into town and came within a hair of capturing Stonewall himself.

This cavalry force consisted of two guns of *Battery L, 1st Ohio Artillery* and 150 members of the *1st West Virginia Cavalry*, all under the command of Col. Samuel S. Carroll. Carroll, commanding Shields' advance brigade, had been ordered on 4 June to proceed from Conrad's Store to Port Republic and seize the bridge there. Because of the heavy rains he had been unable to gather his force together to make the movement, so it was postponed. Three days later, on the 7th, he was directed to march to Port Republic and destroy the bridge there, as well as Jackson's trains that were reported to be parked there. If the movement were successful as planned, Jackson would be stranded in front of Frémont on the north side of the North River. Carroll left Conrad's Store on the afternoon of the 7th with 1000 infantry, 150 cavalry and a six-gun battery. He halted for the night six miles north of Port Republic, and advanced into the town with his cavalry early the next morning. Carroll had no trouble dispersing the Confederate cavalry pickets east of the South River. He then continued on to the lower ford of the South River at Port Republic. Here he posted two guns to dominate the bridge, and sent his cavalry to take possession of the span. He did not doubt he could accomplish this goal because he saw in town only a few Confederate cavalry, the enemy trains, and a large herd of beef cattle. Had he known that Jackson was in town at Dr. Kemper's with no guard, Carroll would surely have focused his attention on the upper end of Port Republic, not the lower.

As it was, Jackson miraculously managed to escape across the North River. He had fortunately received two quick warnings of Carroll's arrival—one from a panicky courier, and another via a screeching Union shell that landed in town. Stonewall immediately sent Jed Hotchkiss to alert the wagons. He and the rest of the staff then mounted up for a mad dash to the bridge. They passed through a sprinkling of Yankee bullets and won their race by a hair. Col. Stapleton Crutchfield and Lieutenant Edward Willis were not so lucky. They lagged a little behind their leader and were captured by Carroll's cavalry. [Crutchfield was later left in town when the Federals retreated. Willis was taken part way back by his captors, but he managed to trick and capture his solitary guard, and then brought the Yankee back with him to Port Republic.]

Though Jackson had escaped to the north side of the river, the excitement in the little town of Port Republic was far from over. Carroll placed two cannon at the base of Main Street, one raking the bridge and the other aimed straight up Main Street. He then dug in to await reinforcements to help him hold his prize.

Meanwhile, a portion of Carroll's cavalry was rushing to grab Jackson's trains that were parked on the far side of the Kemper estate. The only unit actually guarding the trains was Carrington's newly raised Virginia battery of six guns. Carrington's men had never fired a shot in battle, and it is questionable whether they would have stayed to fight had they not been bolstered by a 12-man infantry detachment under Capt. S. C. Moore. Moore's command was supposed to be guarding the upper of the two fords over the South River at Port Republic. When he heard the commotion of Carroll's first foray, Moore rushed over to Kemper's home to get instructions from Jackson or his staff. By then Jackson had already flown the coop.

Fortunately for the Confederates, Moore boldly chose to form his men in a defensive posture at the Kemper estate. His decision was obviously influenced by the fact that Kemper had around his property a panel fence whose four sides made a veritable fort; any Yankees who approached the trains would have to pass right by Kemper's. The approach of the hard riding Yankee cavalry brought enormous confusion to the wagon masters and camp followers in the train parks. Teamsters scurried to hitch up their horses and began stampeding out the Staunton road. Moore's small squad averted what might have been a major disaster by firing a point blank volley into the unsuspecting Federal cavalrymen. A portion of Carrington's command then took heart, pulled up a cannon, and aimed it at

Capt. William T. Poague's battery helped recapture the critical bridge at Port Republic from Carroll's raiding Union troops.

the Yankees. The only problem was that Kemper's plank fence stood before the cannon's mouth. There was no time to knock it down. Carrington's men fired their gun and blew a hole in the fence. Splinters went flying everywhere. The shot missed its mark, but its blast stopped the amazed cavalrymen in their tracks. While the Yankees hesitated, two more of Carrington's guns joined the fray. The Yankees decided they had had enough of the enemy artillery and promptly withdrew back into town.

Meanwhile, Jackson barely paused to catch his breath after dashing across the North River bridge. He knew that he was in dire danger of losing the bridge, his whole army, and the campaign. He rode up to the first troops he saw, Poague's Rockbridge Battery, and ordered it to move closer to the bridge. He then rushed over to Winder's infantry brigade and ordered it to hasten into Port Republic.

Jackson now returned to the north end of the bridge in order to deploy the troops he had just ordered up. He then had an

Federal troops preparing to go into action at Cross Keys. One historian called this engagement a "rambling skirmish" instead of a battle.

interesting confrontation with the crew of one of Carroll's guns, as related later by Poague, "Gen. Jackson finding one of my guns ready to move, directed me to hasten with it towards Port Republic, he himself going along and posting it in the field overlooking and commanding the bridge. I was surprised to see a gun posted at the farther end of the bridge. For I had just come from army headquarters, and, although I met a cavalryman who told me the enemy were advancing up the river, still I did not think it possible they could have gotten any guns into the place in so short a time. It thereupon occurred to me that the gun at the bridge might be one of Carrington's, who was on that side and whose men had new uniforms something like those we saw at the bridge. Upon suggesting this to the general, he reflected a moment, and then riding a few paces to the left and front of our piece, he called in a tone loud enough to be heard by them, 'Bring that gun up here!' but getting no reply, he raised himself up in his stirrups and in a most authoritative and seemingly angry tone he shouted, 'Bring that gun up here, I say!' At this they began to move the trail of the gun so as to bring it to bear on us, which when the general perceived, he quickly turned to the officer in charge of my gun and said, in his sharp, quick way, 'Let 'em have it!' The words had scarcely left his lips when Lieut. Brown, who had his piece charged and aimed, sent a shot right through them, so disconcerting them that theirs in reply went far above us, and in a few minutes, seeing our infantry approaching, they left the place, and, as I was informed, abandoned their gun before crossing South River."

Jackson then ordered the 37th Virginia to charge and take the bridge. The regiment had come up on its own at the sound of the firing, and was eager to please Stonewall. The men had no time or room to deploy into battle line, so they rushed the bridge in column formation. The Yankee gun that Jackson had just confronted blasted a round that shook the sides of the bridge. The 37th lost only a few men from the shot and raced on to storm the gun. The Virginians at once captured the piece, since it had no supporting troops, and turned it on its former owners. Carroll saw the writing on the wall and hurriedly withdrew his whole force across the South River. From start to finish his raid had taken but an hour.

Jackson's batteries north of the South Fork kept up a steady shelling of Carroll's cavalry as the Yankees galloped off to the east. To prevent a repetition of Carroll's raid, Stonewall ordered Taliaferro's brigade to occupy Port Republic. He also sent Winder's brigade two miles downstream to keep lookout for the rest of Shields' command.

The Battle of Cross Keys

While Jackson was dealing with Carroll's incursion at Port Republic, a major battle was developing on Ewell's front at Cross Keys. Frémont was aware that Jackson was at Port Republic, and he had been in contact with Shields, whom he knew was approaching Jackson's position from the east. Therefore he determined to put pressure on Ewell's line at Cross Keys on the morning of 8 June. Frémont's 10,000 men outnumbered Ewell's force about two to one, and he was hopeful of overcoming Ewell before Jackson's division could come up to help.

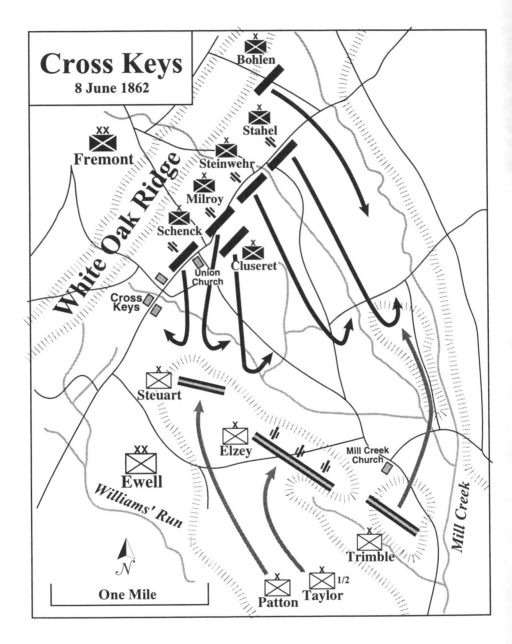

Cross Keys
8 June 1862

Bohlen

Stahel

XX
Fremont

Steinwehr

Milroy

Schenck

Cluseret

White Oak Ridge

Union
Church

Cross
Keys

Steuart

Elzey

Mill Creek
Church

XX
Ewell

Williams' Run

N

Mill Creek

Trimble

One Mile

Patton

Taylor 1/2

The center of the Union battle line at Cross Keys. Frémont should have waited until his entire command had arrived before starting his attack.

Ewell's position was astride the Port Republic-Harrisonburg Road about a mile southeast of the hamlet of Cross Keys and four miles northwest of Port Republic. Ewell's best and largest brigade, Taylor's, was to be loaned to Jackson for the day. He had posted his three remaining brigades on a wooded ridge that could be approached only through cleared fields. Ewell's center was held by five batteries supported by Elzey's brigade. The left, held by Steuart's brigade (formerly Scott's), had additional protection from a stream that ran across its front. The weakest part of Ewell's line was his right, where the woods were so heavy that brigade commander Isaac Trimble felt confined and even vulnerable to a flank attack. For this reason, Trimble sought and received permission from Ewell to advance to a more advantageous position on a ridge a half mile to his right front. There he formed three of his regiments, the 16th Mississippi, 21st Georgia, and 15th Alabama, his fourth, the 21st North Carolina, having been left behind to support the cannon in Ewell's center.

Col. Gustav V. Cluseret's *Advance Brigade*, Frémont's vanguard, reached Cross Keys first and formed near Union Church, skirmishing steadily with the Rebels. As the remainder of Frémont's force came up, he formed them on White Oak Ridge, which ran roughly parallel to Ewell's line about a mile to the southeast. Frémont placed Brig. Gen. Julius Stahel's mostly

German *1st Brigade* on the left near Pirkey's Farm; the brigades of Milroy and Schenck were assigned the army's right wing, and Brig. Gen. Henry Bohlen's *3rd Brigade* was held in the center as a reserve. Frémont's final brigade, von Steinwehr's of Blenker's division, was not yet on the field when the battle started.

The battle of Cross Keys began sometime after 0900 with a brisk exchange of artillery fire. Frémont's plan was to attack first with Stahel's *1st Brigade* on the left; this was a strange decision in view of the fact that most of Stahel's men were then in their first battle, and Frémont had much more experienced troops on the field, particularly in Milroy's and Schenck's brigades, which had fought at McDowell. At about 1000 hours Stahel began advancing across the open fields that separated him from Trimble's position. Upon entering the woods on the far side of these fields, he met and drove back Trimble's skirmishers. Soon thereafter he came upon the main line of the enemy. Here the regiments of his brigade became separated. The *8th* and *45th New York* struck the center of Trimble's line, while the *27th Pennsylvania* and the *DeKalb Regiment* (the *41st New York*) drifted to the right in the woods. The *8th* and *45th* were the first to strike the enemy's line. They apparently advanced without skirmishers, and suffered terribly when Trimble's men held their fire for one devastating close volley. Trimble said of the action, "I ordered the three regiments to rest quietly in the edge of an open wood until the enemy, who were advancing in regular order across the field and hollow, should come within 50 steps of our line. The order was mainly observed, and as the enemy appeared above the crest of the hill a deadly fire was delivered along our whole front, beginning on the right, dropping the deluded victims of Northern fanaticism and misrule by the score."

Stahel's two regiments, the *8th* and *45th New York*, fought valiantly to maintain their line, but soon had to withdraw. The *41st New York*, which was fighting in its first battle, met less severe fire because of its position in the heavy woods. Nevertheless, it and the *27th Pennsylvania* were forced to fall back under close enemy pressure. The pursuing Rebels were checked by Brig. Gen. Henry Bohlen's *3rd Brigade*, which Frémont soon committed to the fray. Bohlen's stand permitted Stahel's men to

Soldiers of the **DeKalb** **Regiment (41st NY),** *who saw their first combat at Cross Keys. Their attack was easily repulsed by Trimble and Ewell.*

escape to their original position, where they attempted to reform.

After a brief lull, the fighting resumed with the initiative now in Confederate hands. Trimble had been reinforced by the 13th and 25th Virginia Regiments, which he placed on his right. He then moved forward against a Union battery one half mile to his front that formed the extreme left of the Union line. Col. Carnot Posey of the 16th Mississippi did not watch his left carefully enough during the advance, with the result that he received stiff fire from Union units in that quarter. These Yankees were then driven off by the 21st Georgia. Farther to the right, the 13th and 25th Virginia Regiments found themselves for a time under the brisk flanking fire of a Federal battery. Nevertheless, they continued their advance, forcing the Yankees to retreat. Trimble's 15th Alabama had the interesting experience of charging up a hill at a Union battery, only to see the battery move off before they got to it. It seems that Frémont was fearful of his left flank being enveloped, so he withdrew the entire flank to a better position. The aggressive Trimble now wanted to keep pressing Frémont's left, but Ewell wisely held him back. Ewell knew he was badly outnumbered on the field and he did not want to overextend his success. In addition, two of Ewell's brigade commanders, Elzey and Steuart, had been wounded, and Trimble's men had been much disorganized by their advance.

Ewell also had to look to the rest of his line. In the center, Union Brig. Gen. Robert Milroy had begun an attack with his brigade which only succeeded in pushing back Ewell's skirmishers. This attack was supposed to keep Ewell from reinforcing the Confederate right, but it failed miserably as Ewell was able to shift the 13th and 25th Virginia regiments of Elzey's brigade to reinforce Trimble.

About 1300 hours Frémont began a belated attack on Ewell's left with Brig. Gen. Robert C. Schenck's brigade, which had just arrived on the field. The Federals managed to drive back the 44th Virginia, but were then checked by Ewell's last reserves, the 12th Georgia and 31st Virginia. A short while later, Ewell's left received additional reinforcements in the form of Patton's brigade and Taylor's 7th and 8th Louisiana Regiments, which an anxious Jackson had forwarded to Ewell from the Port Republic area. These reinforcements took away Schenck's punch, and Schenck soon withdrew because of the defeat suffered on the army's left. At the end of the day, Frémont withdrew his entire command, and Ewell occupied the line the Union army had held at the start of the battle.

Thus ended the battle of Cross Keys, which has been called by one historian a "rambling skirmish." Frémont had been soundly defeated by a much smaller Confederate force because he did not coordinate his attacks. In his battle report, however, Frémont blamed the loss on "the position of uncommon strength" held by the enemy. The Confederate victory was also aided by Ewell's managerial skills, and by Jackson's wisdom in sending unrequested reinforcements at just the right moment. Union losses at the engagement amounted to 557 men killed and wounded and 100 missing or captured; Ewell's losses were only 288 from all causes.

On the evening of 8 June, Trimble continued pressing Ewell to make a night attack on Frémont. Trimble had no respect at all for the Yankee regiments he had faced during the day, and he was certain that they would run again if pressed. Ewell refused to consider such an attack for fear that it would disturb Jackson's plans, but he did allow Trimble to go to meet with Stonewall. Jackson, whether out of weariness or out of respect for Ewell, referred the decision back to Ewell. "Old Baldy" again refused the attack, and his division settled down for the night.

Jackson Plans a Surprise

While Ewell was engaging Frémont, Jackson was keeping an anxious eye on Shields. Shields had begun to advance additional troops at the same time that Frémont attacked Ewell and Jackson feared that the two Union leaders were cooperating in their efforts. As the day wore on Stonewall was concerned about why Shields was not being more aggressive. He knew that if he sat still the next day, he would definitely have to face a battle on two fronts. His remaining lines of action were two—to withdraw, or to attack the enemy. Jackson boldly determined to attack, not just one enemy, but both. His control of the North River bridge made it possible for him to transfer troops from one front to the other, while his opponents did not have this advantage. Since Shields had the smaller force, Jackson decided to attack him on the morning of the 9th, and then transfer his whole force across the river and defeat Frémont. If anything went wrong with the attack on Shields, Frémont could be easily blocked at the North River bridge while Jackson's whole command withdrew safely to the southwest to Brown's Gap. On the other hand, if Frémont were attacked first and something went wrong, Jackson would be in great trouble if Shields put pressure on the only Confederate retreat route over the Port Republic bridge.

Jackson's plan to fight two battles on the same day was a bold one even under the best of conditions. To be certain, he could reasonably count on Frémont being relatively unaggressive, as he had been for much of the campaign. In his planning, though, Jackson failed to take into account the fact that his own troops were exhausted and had undergone many recent command changes. The most unpredictable element of his plan was the fact that the two rivers he would have to cross were rain swollen and unreliable—the North River bridge had been severely shaken during the fighting on the morning of 8 June, and the South River had no bridge, only two fords near the town. Dealing with these factors were key elements in Jackson's plan, which would demand speed and precision in order to be executed successfully.

It was some time after dark on 8 June that Jackson formulated his plan for the double battle on the next day. Orders were sent out to Trimble to hold back Frémont with his own and Patton's brigades; Taliaferro was to hold Port Republic and the heights nearby. This left Jackson with four brigades, the Stonewall Brigade (Winder's), Taylor's, Steuart's, and Elzey's, to use in the attack on Shields. These troops totaled about 8000 men against Shields' 3000. At 0200 on the 9th, Jackson, who was up most of the night making final plans, told Colonel Patton that he hoped to deal with Shields and then be back on the north side of the North River by 1000 hours.

The first, and key, element of Jackson's plan was to erect a useable bridge over the South River at Port Republic. Two fords were near the town, but they were so rain swollen that too much time would be lost fording them. Shortly before midnight Stonewall personally supervised his engineers as they built a makeshift bridge over the South River. He ordered the sides to be pulled off wagons and the wagon beds to be laid end to end across the river. The beds were then connected by boards from a nearby saw mill. The whole device was a shaky affair at best, little suited for its important assignment the next day.

Affairs were already getting off to a bad start as Jackson settled down for an uncomfortable sleep from 0200 to 0600. Several of his units were experiencing difficulty getting fresh ammunition supplies in the dark. In addition, the wagons not used in constructing the South River bridge were slow in moving out of Port Republic. Some had not cleared town when Jackson's infantry began filing through the village before dawn. This created a bottleneck that would last most of the morning, slowing all movements into and out of town.

The Battle of Port Republic

The first infantry unit to begin moving on 9 June was Winder's Stonewall Brigade. Winder was awakened at 0345 with orders to move his brigade into Port Republic within an hour. Arriving there on time, he was directed to cross the South River. The flimsy wagon bridge was so shaky that "a good deal of time was lost in getting the troops over." Winder did not know what his objective was until he met Stonewall himself on the far bank. Jackson guided his old brigade forward, reinforced now by Poague's and Carpenter's batteries. It was 0700 before they reached the Federal skirmishers. Jackson's timetable was already off schedule, and he would now have to push his men extra hard in order to defeat Shields and rejoin Trimble and Patton by 1000 hours.

The force opposing Jackson consisted of 3000 men in eight regiments of Brig. Gen. Erastus B. Tyler's *3rd Brigade* and Col. Samuel S. Carroll's *14th Brigade*; the Yankees also had 16 cannons and the detachment of the *1st West Virginia Cavalry* that had so startled Jackson the day before. The Union force occupied a strong position perpendicular to the South Fork and the Port Republic road, about a mile east of that village. The Union right wing-the *1st West Virginia, 7th Indiana,* and *5th, 7th,* and *29th Ohio* was anchored on the river, while the left—the *84th* and *110th Pennsylvania* and *66th Ohio*—was posted in a dense woods southeast of the Port Republic road. Artillery was strategically placed along the whole front, sweeping the mile of open sloping fields that any Confederate advance would have to cross. Tyler and Carroll expected the arrival of Shields and the rest of his division at any moment. They apparently were not alert to Jackson's movements until just before the battle began.

Jackson was uncertain of the exact size and disposition of the Union force; nevertheless he began the battle as soon as Winder's men came up. Winder advanced his skirmishers as far as he could until they were stalled by enemy artillery fire. Jackson then ordered the 5th and 27th Virginia Regiments, plus two of Poague's guns, to hold the roadway while Col. J. W. Allen led the 2nd and 4th Virginia Regiments in an attack on the Union left.

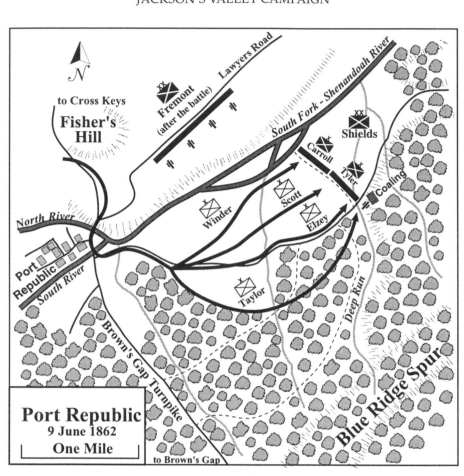

Port Republic
9 June 1862
One Mile

As it developed the battle did not go at all well for the Confederates. Allen experienced great difficulty advancing through the dense woods in which the Federal left rested. This woods was so obstructive that Captain Carpenter had to give up trying to move his guns through the tangle. Allen aimed his march toward a Union battery he could hear more than see. When he reached the battery's front, his scouts observed that the guns were supported by an infantry force larger than Allen's command. Allen responded by sending sharpshooters forward to pick off the cannoneers. As soon as the sharpshooters opened fire, the cannon responded with grape-shot blasts that scattered Allen's whole force.

The Stonewall Brigade was now stalled in its tracks. Allen's two regiments were pinned down on the right, and Winder's other two regiments were likewise being held along the Port Republic road. Winder looked desperately for reinforcements, but none were in sight. His fifth regiment, the 33rd Virginia, had been on picket when he first left the north side of the river in the morning's darkness; by the time it reached Port Republic, it was caught up in the traffic jam in the town and at the bridge. Col. John Neff of the 33rd later told of the confusion that accompanied his movement, "Some time after sunrise on the morning of the 9th I was directed by Lieutenant Garnett to draw in my picket and join my brigade at once. On inquiring where the brigade was, he replied that he was not sure whether it was on the Brown's Gap road or whether it would go down the river. I had scarcely collected my regiment and started for the river when our artillery opened upon the enemy's camp. I pushed on, but before I got to the bridge I found the way blocked by wagons, ambulances, artillery and infantry; it was with great difficulty and considerable loss of time that I at last got my regiment across the main bridge, and encountered almost every obstacle in crossing the temporary one across the smaller stream. I was without any definite knowledge as to the whereabouts of the brigade, but took it for granted it was somewhere on the battlefield, and I moved on in the direction of the regiments which had crossed before me."

Jackson now realized the desperateness of the situation. All hope of beating both Shields and Frémont in the same day was long gone, and he was now in dire danger of losing the battle now before him, against Shields. Because of the congestion in Port Republic, Taylor's brigade also was slow in coming up. If Shields acted quickly, he might attack and overwhelm Winder's four struggling regiments. To relieve the situation, Jackson completely gave up his plans to face Frémont that day. Taliaferro's brigade was ordered to move to support Winder, and Trimble was directed to cross the North River and burn both bridges at Port Republic. This would keep Frémont at a safe distance while Jackson threw his whole force against Shields in an attempt to win at least one victory that day. However, if Trimble withdrew too quickly, Frémont would be able to plant his guns on the bluffs across the river from Shields' position and strike Jackson's lines with enfilading artillery fire that would drive the Confederates off the field.

Despite Jackson's change in plans the crisis for the Confederacy did not immediately improve. Winder desperately needed artillery support, but most of Jackson's cannon had no shells due to the resupply mix-up that had occurred during the night. When Colonel Neff finally brought up the 33rd Virginia, he did not know what to do: "Marching along the road I was considerably annoyed by the enemy's shells, which were bursting in and over the road almost constantly. I got under shelter of a small skirt of wood near the road and pushed on under this cover for some distance, when I came up to an ambulance which the driver told me belonged to the Second Virginia Infantry and from him I learned that the Second Regiment had gone up the same road upon which I was then moving. I continued to march in that direction, expecting to meet with General Winder or some of his aides. At all events I was getting nearer the scene of conflict, where I expected to be of some service. I had gone, as I supposed, half a mile farther, when I met several members of the Fourth Virignia, who told me the regiments were falling back, and their regiment was ordered back to support Carpenter's battery, I was now in the woods; there was sharp firing in front of me; I was totally ignorant of our position of that of the enemy, and scarcely knew what to do. I accordingly halted the regiment and rode forward to ascertain, if possible, something of the condition of affairs. I had proceeded but a short distance when I met Elzey's brigade coming back, and was told upon inquiry, that they could get no position ahead and were coming back to a better one; I could get no information from the First Brigade. In this dilemma I concluded to fall in with Elzey's brigade, and sent Major Holliday to report to Colonel Walker until I could hear positively and know what to do."

It was during this crisis that Taylor began arriving with his large brigade. He had not waited for orders, but began marching to the sound of the guns as soon as the battle opened. Jackson was, to say the least, relieved to see Taylor coming. He immediately sent the 7th Louisiana to bolster the line of the 5th and 27th Virginia, and sent the rest of the brigade to assault the Federal left.

It took time for Taylor's brigade to reach the Union left, almost too much time. In order to keep the Yankee line busy, Winder ordered the three regiments on the Confederate left to attack, even though their Union opponents had superiority of numbers and position, being firmly in line behind a fence. Winder's brave units-the 5th and 27th Virginia and 7th Louisiana-withstood a withering enemy fire and even managed to push back Shields' far right regiment, the *7th Indiana*. When Shields threw the *29th, 7th*, and *5th Ohio Regiments* into the fight, Winder's line had to halt under cover of a fence about 200 yards from the Union line. For three quarters of an hour Winder faced "an option of difficulties," for his men could neither break the Union line, nor give way and face the withering enemy fire. Finally, Rebel courage began to waver as their ammunition began to run out and their lines thinned.

Shields saw Winder's line waver and sent his men forward to drive the Rebels back. Winder desperately threw in his only reserve, the newly arrived 31st Virginia of Elzey's brigade. Still the Yankees kept coming. One of Poague's guns bravely turned to fire another round, only to be captured by the *5th Ohio*. Jackson committed to the fray yet another newly arrived regiment, Steuart's 52nd Virginia, only to see it, too, take flight.

Shields' force might then have swept the field, had not Dick Ewell stepped in to stem their tide. Ewell had been directed by Jackson to lead Steuart's 44th and 58th Virginia Regiments to the fight on the Confederate right. However, as Ewell was coming up he saw the desperate situation on the left and boldly changed his objective. His two small regiments hit the Federal flank and drove it back. Though Ewell's charge was soon repulsed, for the moment he had blunted Shields' counterattack and thus gave Winder a little much-needed breathing space.

Taylor's attack was finally reaching its objective. It had taken him nearly an hour to reach the strongly posted Yankee right, at an old coaling (coal pit) atop a wooded ridge. "Our approach, masked by timber, was unexpected." Taylor would later write in his memoirs, "The battery was firing rapidly, enabled from elevation to fire over the advancing lines. The head of my column began to deploy under cover for attack, when the sounds of battle to our rear appeared to recede, and a loud

Confederate Brig. Gen. Richard Taylor was the son of President Zachary Taylor. By the end of the campaign his Louisiana brigade supplanted the Stonewall brigade as Jackson's shock troops.

Federal cheer was heard, proving Jackson to be hard pressed. It was rather an anxious moment, demanding instant action. Leaving a staff officer to direct my rear regiment—the 7th, Col. Hays—to form in the wood as a reserve, I ordered the attack, though the deployment was not completed, and our rapid march by a narrow path had occasioned some disorder. With a rush and a shout the gorge was passed and we were in the battery. Surprise had aided us, but the enemy's infantry rallied in a moment and drove us out."

Taylor's men were not about to give up their prize cannons without vengeance. As they were being driven back by the *7th* and *5th Ohio Regiments*, several Louisiana Tigers, including their commander, Maj. Robert Wheat, cut the throats of the battery horses so that the guns could not be removed. Then, retreating temporarily, Taylor's men kept up such a fire that the Yankees could withdraw only one of the contested field pieces, though the rest were soon in play again.

Taylor was not about to let the rest of the pieces sit there without another try at them. After a few moments he ordered a second charge. It was a mad affair. As the brush was too thick for the Confederates to form a battle line, they attacked in small bands. "The fighting in and around the battery was hand to hand, and many fell from bayonet wounds," Taylor reported, "Even the artillerymen used their rammers in a way not laid down in the manual, and died at their guns."

Taylor's Tigers retreated a second time, only to rally and make a third attempt. A force of Yankees that had been pouring a raking fire into Taylor's flank was dealt with by two companies of the 9th—Louisiana, who sneaked up a gorge behind them. This charge reached the top of the ridge, where more desperate hand-to-hand fighting followed. Finally it was the Yankees who retreated, leaving behind five of their six guns.

Taylor's men barely had time to catch their breath, when they saw blue-clad reinforcements coming at them from the left. The collapse of Winder's line on the Confederate left had freed several Union regiments to reinforce their hard pressed left at the coaling. Taylor observed, "Wheeling to the right with colors advanced, like a solid wall he marched straight upon us. There seemed nothing left but to set our backs to the mountain and die hard."

Taylor was ready to meet his maker, when a terrible noise came crashing through the underbrush from behind. It was none other than Dick Ewell, who had outstripped his escort as he brought the 44th and 58th Virginia regiments flying to aid Taylor. A few moments later three regiments under Colonel Walker also came to Taylor's aid. Jackson's long delayed reserves were at last reaching the field in time to turn the tide of battle.

Jackson's reinforcements turned the battle on the Confederate left flank as well, where Winder's command had been even more hard pressed than the units in the Confederate center. Winder had seen Shields shifting troops towards the coaling on the Union left, so he raised his weary men to make yet another counterattack. Reinforced by Taliaferro's freshly arrived brigade, Winder's units broke Shields' right and began driving it back. The Union line, which had been in combat for four straight hours, now buckled and caved in along its entire length. At the coaling, Taylor's Louisianians turned the captured guns on their fleeing foes; Jackson himself rode over to the coaling to shake Taylor's hand and promise the guns to his men. Taylor later recalled, "I thought the men would go mad with cheering, especially the Irishmen. A huge fellow, with one eye closed and half his whiskers burned by powder, was riding cockhorse on a gun, and, catching my attention, yelled out, 'We told you to bet on your boys.'"

Winder and Taliaferro pursued Shields' retreating regiments for about five miles. Munford's cavalry then took up the pursuit for another three miles. The chase netted some 450 prisoners, several wagons, one cannon, and 800 muskets. This brought total casualties for the Federals to about 1000, half of them captured. Confederate casualties—almost all due to combat—were over 800, compared to about 500 Union combat losses. Clearly, Shields' two brigades had put up a valiant stand in spite of their small numbers. Indeed, had Shields had his whole force on the field instead of just two brigades, Jackson may well have suffered a defeat worse than Kernstown.

In early afternoon Jackson called off the pursuit and regrouped his army east of Port Republic. By now Trimble had rejoined Ewell's division with the two brigades he had been using to stall Frémont. As ordered, Trimble destroyed the North River bridge and the South River wagon bridge after he crossed them. Frémont's army was now unable to cross and aid Shields or attack Jackson. All Frémont could do was line up his cannons on the heights northwest of the South Fork and begin shelling the Port Republic battlefield. This shelling persuaded Jackson to withdraw his men to a safer position in a cove at the base of Brown's Gap, seven miles southeast of Port Republic. As his tired troops marched off it began to rain. Many of the Confederates did not reach their destination until near midnight.

All in all, the victory was not a glorious one for Stonewall Jackson. His hopes of defeating both Shields and Frémont in one day had simply been too much for his campaign-weary brigades to carry out. Jackson had excellent intentions, but simply asked the impossible of his men. Nor did he consider the potential difficulty of depending on a ramshackle footbridge over the South River. Stonewall had entered the battle in haste, without reconnoitering the Union position or strength. He committed his regiments piecemeal as they arrived and in doing so decimated his own best regiments. Had it not been for his ability to discern the key to the enemy position—the battery at the coaling on the Union left—and his determination to continue attacking until he secured it, he would not have won the day.

There is no question that the victory further shattered Jackson's battered troops. His best brigades, Winder's and Taylor's, had been totally fought-out, and it would be some time before they would regain their former strength and tenacity. But the Yankees did not know this. Both Federal armies were soon retreating up the Valley. Shields began withdrawing on the afternoon of the 9th, for fear of being attacked. He was soon ordered by McDowell to return to Luray. Frémont, isolated now by Shields' withdrawal and chastened by his own defeat at Cross Keys, began pulling out of the Port Republic area on the morning of 10 June. He retreated through Harrisonburg, which Munford's cavalry occupied on the 12th, and reached Banks' force at Middletown on 14 June. Also present at Middletown was Maj. Gen. Franz Sigel's command (Saxton's old Harpers Ferry garrison), as the Federals were finally consolidating their forces, though at too late a stage in the campaign to influence its outcome.

Dick Taylor

During the course of the campaign, Jackson came to rely on the "Louisiana Tigers" of Brig. Gen. Richard Taylor's brigade as his shock troops, even more than his own Stonewall Brigade. At Winchester and Port Republic the Tigers were given the toughest assignment on the field and carried the day. At Cross Keys and McDowell the Tigers arrived in time to save the day. One reason the Tigers may have supplanted the Stonewall Brigade temporarily in Jackson's heart was the brigade's sheer size—its 3000 men made it almost twice as large as Winder's brigade, and in fact the Louisiana brigade was the largest in Jackson's army. But size alone was not the brigade's only strong point. It had an outstanding commander in the person of Dick Taylor, excellent discipline, and great enthusiasm, plus an added spark in the wildness and ferocity of the original Louisiana Tigers Battalion.

The commander of the Louisiana brigade, Dick Taylor (1826-1879), one of the most educated and competent commanders in the Confederate Army, was the son of Zachary Taylor, the Mexican War general who served as the twelfth President of the United States. His education included study at Harvard, Yale, and Edinburgh and in France. Taylor's erudition is clearly shown in his style and the number of classical references in his erudite memoirs, *Destruction and Reconstruction, Personal Memoirs of the Late War* (1879).

Taylor began the war as colonel of the 9th Louisiana, which reached Virginia too late to participate in First Bull Run. In October 1861 he

was promoted to brigadier general in charge of the Louisiana Brigade, a post he was rumored to have attained because of his connections in Richmond—he was a former brother-in-law of Jefferson Davis. Taylor showed his mettle early on when the battalion known as "Wheat's Tigers" was added to his command. This unruly band of New Orleans waterfront ruffians was so villainous that no brigade commander wanted it. Taylor himself noted, "General Johnston assigned it to me, despite my efforts to decline the honor of such society." It did not take long for some of the Tigers to run afoul of Taylor's discipline. Several Tigers got rowdy one night after tattoo and were arrested, and more Tigers tried to break them out. Taylor arrested the two ringleaders of the insurrection, courtmartialed them the next morning, and had them shot at sunset. These were the first executions in Lee's army, and served clear notice to the Tigers that Taylor would brook no disobedience.

Taylor's brigade was part of Ewell's division when Ewell joined Jackson's army. Stonewall was soon quite impressed with Taylor's decorum and the discipline of his command. An anecdote tells of Jackson's reaction upon first seeing the Tigers in the Valley. Taylor's brigade, over 3000 strong, neat in fresh clothing of gray with white gaiters, and jaunty in frame, were marching by as Jackson was perched ungracefully upon the topmost rail of a snake fence. "You seem to have no stragglers," he said to Taylor. "Never allow stragglers'" responded Taylor. "You must teach my people," replied Stonewall, "they straggle badly." But just then the Creoles' band started up a waltz. After a contemplative suck on a lemon, Stonewall observed, "Thoughtless fellows for such serious work."

At Winchester Taylor's brigade was given a chance to show its fighting mettle. The Louisianians were assigned to attack and carry a key ridge that dominated the Federal right flank. Taylor led his men forward with parade ground precision. During this movement he felt "an anxiety amounting to pain for the brigade to acquit itself handsomely." This the men did, and their charge carried its objective and helped sweep the Yankees from the field.

Taylor's men also fought well at Front Royal, where they helped stabilize Ewell's faltering left flank. At Port Republic the brigade had the honor of being the second into action, supporting Winder's Stonewall Brigade. Taylor was ordered to assault the key position in the Union line, a battery located on a wooded ridge at the extreme right of the Yankee line. After several charges the position was finally carried and the battle won. Jackson was so pleased with this effort that he immediately rode up to congratulate Taylor and his men personally.

During the Seven Days' Battles Taylor was too ill to participate, though he did command for a time from an ambulance. In respect for his accomplishments in the Valley, Taylor promoted to major general in late July 1862. He was then transferred to Louisiana—where he owned a plantation—as commander of the District of Western Louisiana. His most notable success there came in the early spring of 1864 when he defeated the large army of Maj. Gen. Nathaniel P. Banks, an old adversary from the Valley Campaign, in the Red River Campaign. Banks had attempted to invade northwestern Louisiana with a large army, but was completely outgeneraled by Taylor, especially at Mansfield (8 April 1864) and in the closing stages of Banks' retreat.

For his victory in the Red River Campaign, Taylor was promoted to lieutenant general. In August 1864 he was assigned to command the Department of East Louisiana, Mississippi, and Alabama. Late in the year he briefly commanded Hood's battered Army of Tennessee. He then returned to his former department, where his was one of the last major Confederate armies to surrender. Taylor finally laid down his sword at Citronelle, Alabama, on 4 May 1865.

During the Valley Campaign the Louisiana brigade consisted of four regiments—the 6th, 7th, 8th and 9th Louisiana infantries—plus a separate battalion, the Louisiana Tigers. Of these units the most famous or notorious was the Tigers. This battalion, technically the 1st Louisiana Special Battalion, had been raised along the levees and in the alleys of New Orleans. Many of its members were "filibusterers" who had fought as mercenaries for various foreign countries in the late 1850s. It was a rowdy lot, to say the least. When the "Tigers"—so named from one of their companies, the "Tiger Rifles"—passed through Richmond on their way to the front, their ruffianism, outlandish uniform, and French accent had caught the imagination of the capital's citizens and newspapers. This reputation was glorified even more when the battalion made a wild charge at the opening of the battle of First Bull Run, where many of the men fought with bowie knives and earsplitting screams.

After First Bull Run the battalion was reputed to be so wild that no sane commander wanted anything to do with it. Dick Taylor's first reaction upon hearing that they were assigned to his brigade has already been mentioned. By his stern discipline Taylor at least managed to keep the Tigers somewhat in line. A good relationship with their commander, Maj. Rob Wheat, also helped keep them under control. During the Valley Campaign Jackson and Taylor enjoyed success using the Tigers as skirmishers and for special assignments, sometimes in support of Ashby's equally wild cavalry.

The Tigers lost much of their identity and cohesion after the battle of Gaines' Mill (27 June 1862), where Major Wheat was mortally wounded. Wheat had been the glue that held the outfit together. When he died, no one was able to control the battalion. It was soon dissolved and its members absorbed into other Louisiana units or sent to other duties.

It had not taken long for the entire Louisiana brigade to adopt the Tigers nickname of the 1st Battalion. Many of the Creoles in the brigade were just as high spirited as the original Tigers. They certainly had style, as an anecdote told by Taylor shows. It seems that after the fall of Winchester, "a buxom, comely dame of some five and thirty summers, with bright eyes and tight ankles, and conscious of these advantages" was upset that Jackson's men had arrived too late to catch all the Yankees. "Whereupon, a tall creole from the Teche sprang from the ranks of the 8th regiment, just passing, clasped her in his arms, and imprinted a sounding kiss on her ripe lips, with 'Madame! je n'arrive jamais trop tard.' A loud laugh followed, and the dame, with a rosy face but merry twinkle in her eye, escaped."

The character of the three other regiments in the brigade was ably summarized by Taylor in his memoirs. "The 6th, Colonel Seymour, recruited in New Orleans, was composed of Irishmen, stout, hardy fellows, turbulent in camp and requiring a strong hand, but responding to kindness and justice, and ready to follow their officers to death. The 9th, Colonel Stafford, was from North Louisiana. Planters or sons of planters, many of them men of fortune, soldiering was hard task to which they only became reconciled by reflecting that it was 'niddering' in gentlemen to assume voluntarily the discharge of duties and then shirk. The 8th, Colonel Kelley, was from the Attakapas-'Acadians," the race of which Longfellow sings in 'Evangeline.' A homeloving, simple people, few spoke English, fewer still had ever moved ten miles from their natal cabanas; and the war to them was a 'liberal education,' as was the society of the lady of quality to honest Dick Steele. They had all the light gayety of the Gaul, and, after the manner of their ancestors, were born cooks. A capital regimental band accompanied them, and whenever weather and ground permitted, even after long marches, they would waltz and 'polk' in couples with as much zest as if their arms encircled the supple waists of the Celestines and Melazies of their native Teche. The Valley soldiers were largely of the Presbyterian faith, and of a solemn, pious demeanor, and looked askant at the caperings of my Creoles, holding them to be 'devices and snares.'"

Following Taylor's transfer west, the Tigers brigade was very ably led for two years by Harry Hays, who had been colonel of the 7th Louisiana during the Valley Campaign. One of the brigade's most glorious moments came at Gettysburg on the evening of 2 July 1863, when it almost single handedly captured some Yankee guns on East Cemetery Hill, one of the strongest portions of the Union line, before being driven back by darkness and lack of proper supports. The brigade suffered badly at Spotsylvania (May 1864), where Hays was wounded, and was then consolidated with the remains of the Second Louisiana Brigade (1st, 2nd, 9th, 10th, 14th, and 15th Louisiana Regiments). The combined unit—still called the Tigers—existed with only phantom strength until the war's end.

Jackson and the Seven Days

When Jackson was ordered to leave the Valley and proceed to Richmond on 18 June 1862 it was expected that he would be the salvation of the capital with his fame, skill, and fair-sized army. Jackson also had high expectations for himself and his men when he conferred with Lee on 23 June and helped formulate plans to defeat McClellan's 100,000-man army and drive it from Richmond. The situation certainly invited a man of Jackson's genius. McClellan's army was split into two wings by the swollen waters of the Chickahominy River and its swamps. His left wing, nearly 70,000 strong, was facing Richmond, while his right wing, over 40,000 men under Maj. Gen. Fitz-John Porter, was stationed in an exposed position north of the Chickahominy. Porter's men were waiting the arrival of reinforcements from Fredericksburg, and were at the moment caught in an awkward position with their right flank unprotected and their left unsupported because of the swollen river. Lee's plan was for Jackson, whose arrival was not suspected by the enemy, to hit Porter's right flank while Lee assaulted Porter's front with most of his army. It was a bold plan that required Lee to leave only 25,000 men south of the Chickahominy to hold the Richmond lines; he hoped to crush Porter's 47,000 with over 70000 in Jackson's command and the divisions of A. P. Hill, D. H. Hill, and Longstreet. Everything hinged on Jackson being able to strike Porter's flank and rear on the morning of 26 June. When Jackson assured everyone that he would be in position on time, Lee committed his forces to the attack, despite reservations by Longstreet and some of his other generals.

Jackson, however, was not able to arrive as had promised. Throughout the whole march he had difficulty pushing his men on towards Richmond. The main problem was that he did not have enough railroad cars to carry all his troops from the Valley to the capital. He used most of the cars he had available to transport supplies; the few remaining ones, were used to "leapfrog" all the troops they could carry. Another delay occurred at Gordonsville on 21 June when he held his men back to watch for a rumored Federal advance. And then Jackson did not move all his troops on 22 June because it was a Sunday.

To make up for these delays, Jackson's troops had some hard marching to do on 24 and 25 June, but no worse than they had done numerous times in the Valley. However, nothing seemed to be working in the men's favor. Jackson's famous foot cavalry began their march "slow and without spirit," as historian D. S. Freeman aptly put it. Their progress was impeded by heavy rains that turned the roads to mud and the unbridged streams to raging torrents. As a result, Jackson's men were five miles short of their goal when they encamped near Ashland on the evening of 25 June. Stonewall was so concerned about arriving in time for his scheduled 26 June attack that he stayed up all night and ordered his men to begin marching at 0230.

Despite his plans for the predawn hours of the 26th, Jackson did not get off to a quick start because his men had difficulty getting food and water. By 0900 the column was six hours behind schedule. As the day progressed, Jackson's men became so thirsty that they started straggling. At about 1600, when he still had not reached his attack position, Jackson heard the sound of heavy fighting to the south; A. P. Hill and D. H. Hill, tired of waiting for Jackson's flank attack, had begun a series of costly frontal attacks that resulted in terrible losses at the Battle of Mechanicsville.

In view of the army's failure at Mechanicsville on the 26th, Lee ordered Jackson to make another attempt to get behind the Federal rear at Old Cold Harbor on the 27th. As Jackson advanced, a miscommunication with his guide caused him to take a wrong road. When he finally got into position at 1500, Jackson held his troops back because he saw no combat occurring. What actually had happened was that the other Confederates had begun their attacks, but then called them off when Jackson failed to show up on time. By the time plans were rearranged, the day's general attack did not begin until an hour before sunset. The Confederates suffered grim losses in direct frontal assaults, and managed to win the day only when Hood's Texas Brigade broke the Union lines at dusk.

Three more days of maneuvering followed as Lee tried to catch one or another part of McClellan's force in transit, as the Yankees retreated before him to a new base. During this critical period Jackson continued to show a total lack of the brilliance which had characterized his recent Valley Campaign. On 29 June he failed to press the reconstruction of the Grapevine Bridge over the Chickahominy, a project that was necessary in order for him to keep up the pressure on McClellan's rear. As a result, the bridge was not finished in time for use, and the men lost most of a day waiting on the north side of the river. After a belated crossing, they were only slightly engaged at Allen's Farm on 29 June. The next-day Jackson advanced with vigor in the morning. When he reached the White Oak Swamp bridge, he was faced with the problem of how to cross in the face of enemy fire. At this crisis he simply folded up and went to sleep. When roused later, he acted confused, and then fell asleep at dinner. Then, in the campaign's final battle, at Malvern Hill on 1 July, Jackson was slow moving into position because he had to reconnoiter a way around or through a swamp that blocked his path. Fortunately for his men, he was not then in position to take part in the slaughter that followed when Lee's unsupported infantry charged a solid line of Federal artillery.

Why did Jackson, the hero of the Valley, perform so miserably in the Seven Days Battles? At the time he was accused by some of being drunk, a standard charge of the day; this charge makes no sense in view of Jackson's teetotaling habits. James Longstreet, always Jackson's rival, claimed Jackson fared poorly at Richmond because he was faced with Union generals much more competent than the likes of Banks and Frémont, his principal opponents in the Valley. Others at the time thought that Jackson was reluctant to use up his men in any bloody battles, and he wished to leave the fighting to the less experienced Richmond troops. More re-

cently, kinder-hearted critics have cited Jackson's unfamiliarity with the terrain around Richmond and weaknesses in Confederate staff as causes for Jackson's shortcomings.

The most plausible reason for Jackson's poor performance at Richmond is sheer exhaustion, a theory best put forward by historian Douglas Southall Freeman. In almost every other campaign, Jackson was quick to analyze unfamiliar terrain and master each situation as it arose. In a careful analysis in his acclaimed biography *R.E. Lee*, Freeman shows that Jackson pushed himself beyond endurance from 22-30 June. His daytime hours were filled with strenuous activity, first hurrying to and from the conference with Lee on the 23rd, then pushing his troops to Ashland. Most significantly, Jackson was severely deprived of sleep during that week—on four nights he had no sleep after midnight; and on the other four nights he was up at dawn.

Jackson's exhaustion was noted at the time by Major Dabney, who said that the general was so tired that he literally fell asleep during dinner on 30 June. Another soldier noted that Jackson was not feeling well during the Seven Days Battles: "The truth of the matter is that he and his men had been completely worn out by what they had gone through." Jackson himself admitted to his wife on 8 July that he had not been feeling well, "During the past week, I have not been well, have suffered from fever and debility."

Thus, then, we should probably agree with Freeman that Jackson's poor performance in the Seven Days Battles was due largely to "the lack of calculation of an exhausted mind," a situation that would have compounded the other problems he faced in the swampy flatlands near Richmond.

Historian Robert F. Tanner in his book *Stonewall in the Valley* has taken Freeman's theory a step farther and used it to help explain Jackson's performance in the last week of the Valley Campaign. Here, as at Richmond, Jackson was not at his best, particularly in his overly ambitious plan to defeat both Shields and Frémont on 9 June, and in his poor tactics at Port Republic.

That Jackson was exhausted at the end of the Valley Campaign should appear as no surprise. Ever since he began the dash south from Winchester he had been under constant tension and pressure. By Tanner's reconstruction, Jackson had only one good night's sleep (June 7-8) in the last ten days of the campaign; on three nights (30-31 May, 1-2 June, and 7 June) he was up well past midnight and got little or no sleep; on three or four other nights his sleep was disturbed by rain or by the necessity of rising before dawn. This lack of sleep caused many of Jackson's men, including some of his staff members, to lose their health. Thus it is no wonder that Sandie Pendleton on 7 June observed, "General Jackson is completely broken down."

CHAPTER VIII

Jackson Triumphant

The Valley Campaign had now reached an impasse, as both sides were punched out and awaiting future developments. On 12 June Jackson transferred the army to a "noble park like forest" near Weyer's cave. Here he allowed his troops to relax for an unprecedented five days. On 13 June he issued a congratulatory order, "The fortitude of the troops under fatigue and their valor in action have again, under the blessing of Divine Providence, placed it in the power of the commanding general to congratulate them upon the victories of June 8 and 9. Beset on both flanks by two boastful armies, you have escaped their toils, inflicting successively crushing blows upon each of your pursuers. Let a few more such efforts be made, and you may confidently hope that our beautiful Valley will be cleansed from the pollution of the invader's presence. The major-general commanding invites you to observe to-morrow evening, June 14, from 3 o'clock P.M., as a season of thanksgiving, by a suspension of all military exercises, and by holding divine service in the several regiments."

Jackson longed to resume operations against Frémont and drive the Federals from the Valley. His campaign so far had been a masterpiece and had drained thousands of troops from McClellan's army before Richmond, in addition to putting a scare into Lincoln and all of Washington. Jackson begged Lee—commanding Johnston's army after the latter had been wounded at Seven Pines on 31 May—for reinforcements to make up his losses and enable him to resume the offensive. On

General Irvin McDowell. This thoughtful commander's military decisions were often overruled for political reasons.

11 June, Lee agreed to send three brigades of 8000 men under Brig. Gen. W. H.C. Whiting. In a masterpiece of psychological warfare, Whiting's men were marched through Richmond without disguising their goal.

Jackson was excited to receive these reinforcements, and began to develop plans greater than merely crushing Banks. He promised that if he received another 20,000 men, he would overwhelm all his opponents and carry the campaign into Pennsylvania. This prospect was exciting to Lee and Davis, but in the end Lee's calmer judgment prevailed. McClellan was the major threat to the Confederacy, and he had to be dealt with directly. Jackson would not be reinforced beyond Whiting's division. With this news, Jackson's ardor subsided somewhat. In a reply to Richmond he wrote, "So far as I am concerned, my opinion is that we should not attempt another march down the Valley to Winchester until we are in a condition under the blessing of Providence to hold the country."

For their part, the Yankees were not eager to renew the campaign at all. Lincoln realized too late how his dispersion of forces had allowed Jackson to use his interior lines to great advantage. On 9 June, the day of the battle at Port Republic, Lincoln decided to reactivate his plans to have McDowell attack Richmond from the north. For this purpose he ordered Shields to "cease all further pursuit and bring back all your division to

Luray, and get ready for the march to Fredericksburg." This move was exactly what the generals in Richmond feared, since they did not really have troops available to face McDowell. In fact, McDowell had foreseen that his movement to the Valley in late May was a great mistake, and that he would soon be returning with empty hands to Fredericksburg.

Shields later claimed that he was astounded at the orders to withdraw to Luray. He said that he was preparing, even on the evening of 9 June, to renew his attack on Jackson in conjunction with Frémont. Then, he says, "I received a positive and peremptory order to return to Luray. There was no option left me. I never obeyed an order with such reluctance, but I had to return." Shields, however, appears to have exaggerated the bluntness of the orders he received. A detailed letter from President Lincoln sent him at the same time as the withdrawal order, preserved in the *War of the Rebellion, Official Records of the Union and Confederate Armies*, explained that the defense of the Valley was to be entrusted to Frémont and Banks. These two generals would see to it that "Jackson shall be made to pay for his late dash down the Valley." This communique then went on to state that Shields was being recalled because he seemed to be too far out of touch with his supports; however, if Shields were "in hot pursuit and about to fall on the enemy, and can do so with reasonable chance of success without relying on the troops at Front Royal, . . . the general is not disposed to recall you."

On 9 June Frémont also received orders from President Lincoln to suspend chasing Jackson: "Halt at Harrisonburg, pursuing Jackson no farther. Get your force well in hand and stand on the defensive, guarding against a movement of the enemy either back toward Strasburg or toward Franklin, and await further orders, which will be soon be sent to you." As noted, Frémont began withdrawing down the Valley by stages, followed closely by Munford's cavalry. During his withdrawal, he appears to have been more concerned with finding full rations for his men than with fighting the enemy. In fact, in view of the repeated rumors of Jackson's heavy reinforcements, he may not have wished to face Jackson again until he joined Banks' command at Middletown.

It was only now that Lincoln reorganized western Virginia into a more sensible administration. He assigned Frémont the job of defending most of the Valley, and extended his frontier east to the Massanutten. Frémont was ordered to cooperate with Banks, whose sphere was limited to the lower Valley and the area just east of the Blue Ridge. These arrangements freed McDowell to resume his long delayed advance towards Richmond. Lincoln had at last learned his lesson, as he wrote to Frémont on 15 June, "I think Jackson's game—his assigned work—now is to magnify the accounts of his numbers and reports of his movements, and thus by constant alarms keep three or four times as many of our troops away from Richmond as his own force amounts to. Thus he helps his friends at Richmond three or four times as much as if he were there. Our game is not to allow this."

Even so, Lincoln was not particularly satisfied with this new command arrangement in the Shenandoah. He knew that lack of good central control over the three commands there—Frémont, Banks and McDowell—had helped Jackson escape his trap of late May. Less than two weeks after he organized the new command setup he again altered command arrangements by joining McDowell's, Banks' and Frémont's commands into the *Army of Virginia* under command of a newcomer, Maj. Gen. John Pope, who had had some success on the Mississippi. Pope's assigned objective was to coordinate the defense of the Shenandoah with an offensive towards Richmond.

As Lincoln rearranged his armies in the Valley, Lee decided to take advantage of the suspension of activity. Jackson would not be hurled against the Yankee defenders of Winchester. Instead, he was called to Richmond on 16 June, to help drive off McClellan. As Lee told Davis, "The enemy in the Valley seems at a pause. We must strike them here before they are ready there to move up the Valley. They will naturally be cautious and we must be secret and quick."

On 17 June Jackson and his battle-hardened veterans began leaving the Valley to join Lee's army before Richmond. Their arrival meant much more than their mere numbers. Throughout the spring of 1862, a spring that saw disaster at Shiloh, the loss of New Orleans, and McClellan's ponderous advance up the

Stonewall Jackson was accidentally wounded by some of his own men on the evening of 2 May 1863 at the battle of Chancellorsville. He died eight days later and was buried in Lexington, Va.

Peninsula to Richmond, Jackson and his brilliant victories were the sole light of hope for the Confederacy. In less than three months he had marched over 400 miles, fought five major battles, winning four, defeated three different Union armies, and neutralized almost 100,000 Union troops with a force that never exceeded 17,000.

Truly it had been a marvelous campaign, but not a perfect or preplanned one. At each critical junction Jackson weighed carefully his options, usually—and sometimes too boldly—choosing the most aggressive alternative. At times his plans were simply too aggressive-witness the Romney incursion, the attack at Kernstown, and the proposed double battle at Port Republic on 9 June. He also lacked tactical finesse at times, particularly at Kernstown and Port Republic. But his moments of glory far outshone his shortcomings. His magnificent use of geography, his exploitation of enemy weaknesses and disorganization, and his use of concentrated force (particularly at McDowell and Winchester) made this campaign alone enough to carve the name "Stonewall Jackson" deeply in the annals of military history.

STRATEGY AND TACTICS

One of the primary reasons for Jackson's success in the Valley campaign was his aggressive nature and aggressive strategy. As outlined in the text, he had no overall plan for the campaign when it began other than an appreciation for the fact that his was a theatre secondary to that occupied by the main army defending Richmond. However, being a native of western Virginia, he fully realized the strategic value of keeping a strong presence in the lower Valley. This had multiple goals: to protect the western approaches to Richmond, to keep the entire Valley (with its recruits and supplies) in Confederate control, to block enemy transportation and communications lines along the Baltimore and Ohio railroad and the Chesapeake and Ohio canal, and to threaten Union towns in western Maryland and Pennsylvania. By his aggressive nature, Jackson fully realized that the best way to hold his somewhat exposed position in the face of superior enemy strength was to take the offensive himself. This premise is what lies at the basis of his success in the campaign.

Jackson's aggressiveness and instinct for hitting the enemy where he was least expected led him to success after success: Romney, Kernstown (a tactical defeat but strategic success), McDowell, Winchester, and Cross Keys/ Port Republic. His rapidity and decisiveness of action often made his own luck as he hit enemy weak points and took advantage of indecision and unpreparedness on the part of Union commanders. Often his own principles and maxims gave him added

advantages. His ability to concentrate a superior force at the point of attack, in spite of being outnumbered in the theatre, led to victories at McDowell, Front Royal, Winchester, and Port Republic. His efforts to deceive the enemy as to his intentions worked well at Kernstown (where he feinted a southern movement on the day before the battles before he turned back to fight), McDowell (where his march to Mechum River Station confused even his own troops for awhile), and in his approach to Winchester in late May (where he made use of the geography of the Valley for a time to march part of his force up the main valley and part up the Luray Valley).

As successful as Jackson's strategic aggressiveness was, it sometimes brought him into positions of grave danger. His bold march on Romney in late 1861 was designed to catch the enemy off balance, but he instead ended up exhausting his own troops in extremely bad weather. Jackson's aggressive attack at Kernstown, where he assaulted a force that he did not know outnumbered his own, could well have ended in a major disaster, even though he later called his tactical defeat a strategic victory. After the capture of Winchester on May 25, he rushed his troops forward to try to grab Harpers Ferry and perhaps invade Maryland; but, instead of throwing a scare into the enemy, his drive ran out of steam and was almost cornered. Finally, Jackson's scheme to defeat both Shields and Frémont on June 8 was simply more than his men could handle. It almost caused him to lose the battle of Port Republic.

Jackson's success was also due largely to the fact that he could clearly perceive his goals and then could push his officers and men to achieve them. Though he occasionally had greater ambitions than his men could physically carry out, they came to admire and trust, if not love (or hate) him for his ability to win. Jackson demanded blind obedience from his officers and men alike. Woe to any soldier who questioned Jackson's orders or did not do as was ordered or expected of him—as Dick Garnett found out at Kernstown, and A.P. Hill did later that year during the march to Antietam (Hill did not follow Jackson's orders to prevent straggling, so Jackson placed him under arrest, even though a major battle was imminent).

That Jackson was able to carry out his ambitious plans was in no small measure due to the ability of his staff, which was perhaps the best and most efficient formed by any commander at any level during the war. His staff members were extremely skilled, devoted, and physically strong individuals whom Jackson could and did rely on to carry out his wishes exactly. Especially notable were his transport and supply officers,

Jackson's campaign was a masterpiece of logistics, particularly in his march to McDowell, and when he retreated from Harpers Ferry and Winchester with his prisoners and captured supplies intact. Only once did his logistical system break down, and that was when he did not have his long range artillery at hand for the opening of the battle of

Winchester. This was an unusual slip up; Jackson customarily pushed his ammunition wagons forward even ahead of the provision wagons. His men could forage or even go hungry if they received no rations, but they could not fight without ammunition.

A strange side of Jackson's strategy was his passion for secrecy. He very seldom told his men details of strategic or battle plans beyond what they needed to know to make their own movements. Jackson firmly believed that "If I can deceive my own friends I can make certain of deceiving the enemy." He surely subscribed to Frederick the Great's maxim "If I thought my coat knew my plans, I would take it off and burn it." This intense secrecy did indeed have its merits, particularly in the successful movement against Frémont's troops at McDowell. But it was by all reasonable terms carried to excess. His refusal to tell his own generals his plans led to confusion both on the march (as in the Romney campaign, when his commanders did not know their objective and so were not able to prepare mentally for action) and on the battlefield (witness Garnett's confusion as to his goal at Kernstown and the uncertainty of his troops as they headed into action at Port Republic). On the other hand, when Jackson explained his goals to his generals (as in the attack on Winchester), they came through with spectacular success. The Confederacy was indeed fortunate that nothing happened to incapacitate Jackson at any one of several critical points in the campaign, since none of his subordinates would then have had any idea what the commander's intentions were.

Jackson's sense of battlefield tactics was nowhere as well developed as his feelings for strategy. All too often his aggressive plans led him into battle with, as they say, "only one boot on." At Kernstown he underestimated the size of the enemy force on the field, and then began a flanking movement against the Union right without reconnoitering the ground first; this blind attack soon got stalled against superior numbers on his far left. Jackson was also at fault at Kernstown for sending his biggest brigade (Garnett's) into action with only a part of its force. Jackson held Garnett's largest regiment in reserve, and then personally interfered with the movement of other units in Garnett's command.

Jackson showed poor tactical handling of his troops at McDowell. Here his regiments became intermingled, and his men initially suffered more casualties than the enemy, even though they were fighting on the defensive and so technically had a tactical advantage. Nor did Jackson keep his reserves well in hand at McDowell—he committed them as they came up, and even then did not keep firm control of them.

Jackson's worst tactical battle may well have been Port Republic. Here he once again rushed his troops into action without reconnoitering and in piecemeal fashion as they reached the field. This hastiness almost completely destroyed the Stonewall Brigade, which had suffered severely under much the same conditions at Kernstown. It was only Jackson's uncanny ability to perceive the key to the Union position (the battery at the coaling)

and then press on doggedly until it was taken, that finally won the day.

This is not to say that Jackson did not have strengths as a tactician. He knew well how to use combined arms (infantry, cavalry and artillery) in action, as was demonstrated particularly well at Front Royal and again at Winchester. He also was able to gauge well the strengths and abilities of his generals and units. As the campaign progressed, he came to rely more and more on Taylor's Louisiana brigade as his shock troops in place of his exhausted Stonewall Brigade. He made good use of his Maryland outfits and of Turner Ashby and his unruly command. Jackson learned to place complete faith in his nominal second-in-command, Dick Ewell (particularly at Cross Keys). It was purely to Jackson's advantage, in the end, that the strategical skills he used to ensure numerical superiority on the battlefield were able to more than make up for his tactical lapses. Such was the case at McDowell and Port Republic, and was true in the reverse at Kernstown, where his failure to achieve numerical superiority on the field was unable to compensate for his faulty tactical movements.

Jackson had difficulties with his cavalry. He was an expert at using cavalry for scouting, covering movements, deceiving the enemy, and blocking enemy retreats. However, he was not able to use his cavalry effectively on the battlefield (most notably at the close of the battle of Winchester), nor was he able to keep a firm rein on his largest cavalry unit (Ashby's) or its commander. This difficulty was posed mostly by the cavalier spirit of

Ashby and his men. Jackson permitted them to lead a relatively undisciplined life because they performed their scouting duties so ably; his attempts to enforce more discipline on them, particularly the reassignment of "Maryland" Steuart to cavalry command, failed to achieve his desired goal. In the end, Ashby and his men presented more of a command control problem than Jackson could solve.

A discussion of Jackson's military skills would not be complete without a comment on the training and drill with which he shaped his command. Much of the success of the Stonewall Brigade was due to the sense of discipline Jackson instilled in its men before and after First Bull Run; he used much the same regimen later to train the other troops that formed the Valley Army. He had high expectations of his men, but he also treated them well, seeing that they were properly supplied, fed, and paid. He learned from the Romney winter campaign how low his men's morale could sink when their needs were not properly met, and he took care that such a situation did not arise again. In addition, Jackson's skills as an organizer should not be overlooked, particularly during the critical period of the army's reorganization in the spring of 1862.

Lastly, a few words need to be said about Jackson's marching philosophy. His troops were called "foot cavalry" not just because of the speed with which they usually moved, but also because of the exceptional speed they could attain when they had to, particularly in the approach to Kernstown, the movement on McDowell, and the retreat from Winchester. Jackson trained his men to march at or before dawn (his men often said he always started marching before dawn, except when he started the night before) and developed a peculiar routine to enable them to cover more ground easily. He regularly marched his men hard for 50 minutes each hour and then let them rest for 10 minutes; he properly figured that they would march harder if they knew a rest stop was not far off. Jackson also usually let his men stop for an hour for lunch, as long as the occasion permitted.

Jackson and his foot cavalry indeed did great and memorable deeds in the Shenandoah Valley. But they were not supermen. In the course of the campaign both Jackson and his men became worn out physically and mentally. The legendary speed with which the foot cavalry marched was aided appreciably by the hard surface of the macadamised Valley Turnpike on which they usually marched. Their speed of movement was also enhanced by the fact that Jackson simply demanded—and got—more marching from them than Union leaders expected from their troops.

The fact is that Jackson did not face the best generals and troops fielded by the North. Shields and Williams were decent generals, but the theatre's principal Union commanders, Frémont, Banks, and Blenker, certainly were not the equivalent of Sheridan, McPherson or Hancock. Some of the Union troops were of high quality (particularly those of Banks' command, which later formed the basis of the XIIth/XXth Corps, as solid an outfit as existed in the Union Army), but other troops, notably Frémont's, had a very poor track record (Frémont's men became the nucleus of the *XIth Corps*, which never fought a winning battle and was disgraced at Chancellorsville and Gettysburg). In addition, the inefficient Union command structure, which saw no overall leadership in the theatre until the campaign was virtually over, helped hamstring the numerically superior Northern forces in the Valley.

In the last analysis, however, it was Jackson's peculiar talents and abilities that enabled him to exploit the Union weaknesses just listed. His aggressiveness was ideally suited to face the divided and less competent Union generals who opposed him. It is doubtful if any Confederate general with less than Jackson's genius could have accomplished what Stonewall did with the forces available to him in the Shenandoah Valley in the spring of 1862.

Jackson's "Foot Cavalry"

Jackson's troops were often called "foot cavalry" not just because of the speed with which they usually moved, but also because of the high rate of speed they could attain when they had to, particularly in the approach to Kernstown, the movement on McDowell, and the retreat from Winchester. Jackson trained his men to march at or before dawn (his men often said he always started marching before dawn, except when he started the night before) and developed a peculiar routine to enable them to cover more ground easily. He regularly marched his men hard for 50 minutes each hour and then let them rest for 10 minutes; he properly figured that they would march harder if they knew a rest stop was not far off. Jackson also usually let his men stop an hour for lunch, as long as time permitted. He didn't like to march or fight on Sundays, but often could not avoid doing so.

DATE	CAMP	MILES MARCHED
10 Mar 62	Winchester	—
11 Mar	Strasburg	18
12 Mar	"	0
13 Mar	"	0
14 Mar	"	0
15 Mar	Woodstock	12
16 Mar Sun	Mt. Jackson (part)	12
17 Mar	"	0
18 Mar	"	0
19 Mar	"	0
20 Mar	"	0
21 Mar	Woodstock (all)	12
22 Mar	Strasburg	18
23 Mar Sun	Newtown (Battle of Kernstown)	24
24 Mar	Mt. Jackson	6
25 Mar	"	0
26 Mar	"	0
27 Mar	"	0
28 Mar	"	0
29 Mar	"	0
30 Mar Sun	"	0
1 Apr	Mt. Jackson	0
2 Apr	Rude's Hill	4
3 Apr	"	0
4 Apr	"	0
5 Apr	"	0
6 Apr Sun	"	0

Date	Location	Value
7 Apr	"	0
8 Apr	"	0
9 Apr	"	0
10 Apr	"	0
11 Apr	"	0
12 Apr	"	0
13 Apr Sun	"	0
14 Apr Sun	"	0
15 Apr	"	0
16 Apr	"	0
17 Apr	Near Harrisonburg	15
18 Apr	Peale's (southern end of Massanutten Mt.)	16
19 Apr	Elk Run Valley (between Conrad's Store and Swift Run Gap)	12
20 Apr Sun	"	0
21 Apr	"	0
22 Apr	"	0
23 Apr	"	0
24 Apr	"	0
25 Apr	"	0
26 Apr	"	0
27 Apr Sun	"	0
28 Apr	"	0
29 Apr	"	0
30 Apr	Between Conrad's Store and Port Republic	7
1 May	2 miles from Port Republic	5
2 May	Between Port Republic and Brown's Gap	5
3 May	Mechum's Station	15
4 May Sun	Railroad to Staunton (part)	—
5 May	Staunton (all)	(22)
6 May	Staunton	0
7 May	Dry Branch Gap	16
8 May	McDowell–Battle of McDowell	14
9 May	McDowell	0
10 May	Road to Franklin	12
11 May Sun	Near Franklin	10
12 May	Near Franklin	0
13 May	Road to McDowell	10
14 May	McDowell	10
15 May	Lebanon–White Sulphur Springs	15
16 May	National Day of Fasting and Prayer	0

17 May	Bridgewater, near Mt. Solon	17
18 May Sun	"	0
19 May	Dayton, en route to New Market	6
20 May	New Market	20
21 May	East side of New Market Gap	7
22 May	10 miles south of Front Royal	13
23 May	Crooked Run	15
24 May	Newtown	7
25 May Sun	Stephenson's Depot	11
26 May	Stephenson's Depot	0
27 May	"	0
28 May	Stephenson's Depot (5 miles from Charlestown-Winder)	11
29 May	Halltown (part)	17
29 May	Halltown (Winder)	6
30 May	Winchester	20
31 May	Strasburg	19
1 June Sun	Edinburg	14
2 June	Mt. Jackson	10
3 June	New Market	6
4 June	Harrisonburg	14
5 June	Port Republic	12
6 June	"	0
7 June	"	0
8 June Sun	Port Republic	0
9 June	Brown's Gap (Battle of Port Republic)	12
10 June	Brown's Gap	0
11 June	"	0
12 June	Weyer's Cave	8
13 June	"	0
14 June	"	0
15 June Sun	"	0
16 June	"	0
17 June	Off to Richmond	

Orders of Battle

The Principal Valley Engagements

Due to fragmentary documentation it is difficult to establish the precise composition and strength of the forces involved in the principal battles in the Valley Campaign. The figures which follow are based on a careful examination of the available evidence supplemented by some educated deductions. Normally the number of troops is given for each brigade, with total of killed, wounded, and missing/captured. Wherever possible, figures have been provided for lower level units as well. In addition, it has occasionally proven possible to determine the types of pieces used by individual artillery units and these have been indicated as appropriate. As a result, these figures are the most comprehensive ever published.

To facilitate the presentation of the orders of battle a number of conventions have been adopted. State abbreviations have been used and the ordinal ending has been left off most unit designations. All units are infantry regiments unless otherwise noted. Thus, "29 Oh" is the "29th Ohio Volunteer Infantry Regiment." For the cavalry (Cav), all units are regiments unless otherwise noted. In the artillery (Art), all units are batteries, technically belonging to a state regiment, as shown. Since Civil War practice was to call a battery by its commander's name, this has been given in parentheses. Where only a portion of a unit is known to have been involved, this has been indicated. Abbreviations and symbols used are as follows:

Btty—battery	**m**—missing
(always artillery)	**nr**—not reported
Coy—company	**Sqn**—squadron
c.—approximately	**w**—wounded
Det-detachment	**>**—number is the
	minimum
k—killed	**?**—unknown

	KILLED	WOUNDED	MISSING	TOTAL
Kernstown				
23 March 1862				
Union Forces, c. 7600	118	450	22	590
Brig. Gen. James Shields (w)				
Col. Nathan Kimball				
1st Brigade, c. 2200	45	200	1	246
Col. Nathan Kimball				
14 *Ind*	4	50	0	54
8 *Oh*	11	41	1	53
67 *Oh*	9	38	0	47
84 *Pa*	21	71	0	92
2nd Brigade, c. 2200	23	69	0	92
Col. Jeremiah Sullivan				
39 *Ill*	0	0	0	0
13 *Ind*	5	37	0	42
5 *Oh*	18	32	0	50
62 *Oh*	0	0	0	0
3rd Brigade, c. 2400	43	171	21	235
Col. Erastus D.Tyler				
7 *Ind*	7	33	9	49
7 *Oh*	20	62	10	92
29 *Oh*	3	10	2	15
110 *Pa*	7	43	0	50
1 *WVa*	6	23	0	29
Cavalry Brigade, c. 300	3	6	0	9
Col. Thornton Brodhead				
1 *Pa Cav* (1 sqn)				
Md Cav (2 coys)				
1 *WVa Cav Bn*				
1 *Oh Cav* (A, C Coys)				
1 *Mich Cav* (1 bn)				
Artillery, c.50	4	2	0	6
Lt. Col. Philip Daum				
Btty A, WVa Art (Jenkins)	1	0	0	1
Btty B, WVa Art (?)	0	0	0	0
Btty H, 1st Oh Art (Huntington)	1	0	0	1
Btty L, 1st Oh Art (Robinson)	1	2	0	3
Btty E, US 4th Art (Clark)	1	0	0	1
Signal Detachment, c. ?	0	1	0	1

	KILLED	WOUNDED	MISSING	TOTAL
CONFEDERATE FORCES, c.3200	80	375	287	718
Maj. Gen. Thomas J. Jackson				
Garnett's Brigade, c. 1500	40	168	153	361
Brig. Gen. Richard S. Garnett				
2 Va, 320	6	33	51	90
4 Va, 203	5	23	48	76
5 Va, c. 300	9	48	4	61
27 Va, c. 200	2	20	35	57
33 Va, 275	18	27	14	59
Rockbridge Va Btty, 8 guns & c. 50 (McLaughlin)	0	10	1	11
West Augusta Va Btty, 4 guns & c.90 (Waters)	0	7	0	7
Carpenter's Va Btty, 4 guns & 48	0	0	0	0
Burks' Brigade, c.700	24	114	39	167
Col. Jesse Burks				
21 Va, 270	7	44	9	60
42 Va, 293	11	50	9	70
48 Va, unengaged				
1 Va Bn, 187	6	20	21	47
Pleasant's Va Btty, 4 guns & c.50	0	0	0	0
Fulkerson's Brigade, c.650	15	76	71	162
Col. Samuel Fulkerson				
23 Va, 177	3	14	32	49
37 Va, 397	13	62	39	113
Danville Va Btty, 4 guns & c. 50 (Lanier)	0	0	0	0
Cavalry, c. 340	1	17	0	18
Col. Turner Ashby				
7 Va Cav 290	1	17	0	18
Chew's Va Btty, 3 guns & c.50	0	0	0	0

	McDowell 8 May 1862			
	KILLED	WOUNDED	MISSING	TOTAL
UNION FORCES, c. 6000, 2268 engaged	26	227	3	256
Brig. Gen. Robert Schenck				
Milroy's Brigade, c. 1768 engaged	20	177	3	199
Brig. Gen. Robert Milroy				
25 *Oh*, 469	6	51	1	58
32 *Oh*, 416	4	52	0	56
73 *Oh*, unengaged				
75 *Oh*, 444	6	32	1	39
2 *WVa*, unengaged				
3 *WVa*, 419	4	42	0	46
Btty, I, 1 Oh Art (Hyman), unengaged				
12 Oh Art Btty (Johnson), unengaged				
1 WVa Cav, unengaged				
Schenck's Brigade, c. 750	6	50	1	57
Brig. Gen. Robert Schenck				
55 *Oh*, unengaged				
83 *Oh*, c. 500	6	50	1	57
5 *WVa*, unengaged				
Btty K, 1 Oh Art (DeBeck), unengaged				
1 Conn Cav, c.250	0	0	0	0

	KILLED	WOUNDED	MISSING	TOTAL
CONFEDERATE FORCES, C. 6000	75	423	0	498
Maj. Gen. Thomas J. Jackson				
The Army of the Valley	12	98	0	110
Maj. Gen. Thomas J. Jackson				
2nd Brigade—Col. John Campbell	0	9	0	9
21 Va	0	1	0	1
42 Va	0	3	0	3
48 Va	0	4	0	4

1 Va Btty (?)	0	1	0	1
3rd Brigade—Brig. Gen. William Taliaferro	12	89	0	101
10 Va	1	20	0	21
23 Va	6	35	0	39
37 Va	3	34	0	39
Army of the Northwest	63	325	0	388
Brig. Gen. Edward Johnson (w)				
1st Brigade—Col. Z.T. Conner	43	223	0	266
12 Ga, 540	35	140	0	175
25 Va	7	65	0	72
31 Va	1	18	0	19
2nd Brigade—Col. W.C. Scott	20	62	0	122
44 Va	2	17	0	19
52 Va	7	46	0	53
58 Va	11	39	0	50

The Front Royal / Winchester Operation
23 to 25 May 1862

	KILLED	WOUNDED	MISSING	TOTAL
UNION FORCES, c. 6500	62	243	1714	2019
Maj. Gen. Nathaniel P. Banks				
1st Division	51	201	1287	1541
Brig. Gen. Alpheus Williams				
1st Brigade, 1700—Col. Dudley Donnelly	17	98	735	850
5 *Conn*	1	12	71	84
1 *Md*	14	43	535	592
28 *NY*	0	2	62	64
46 *Pa*	2	43	65	110
3rd Brigade, 2102—Col. George H. Gordon	22	80	507	609
2 *Mass*	13	47	80	140
27 *Ind*	3	17	104	124
29 *Pa*	2	5	237	244
3 *Wis*	4	11	86	101
Cavalry Brigade, 700+—Brig. Gen. John P. Hatch	5	25	294	324
1 *Md Cav*, c. 300	0	0	5	5
1 *Me Cav*	0	1	128	129
5 *NY Cav*, c. 200	4	15	56	75
1 *Vt Cav*, c. 200	1	9	105	115
Miscellaneous, c. 380	12	24	46	82
1 *Mich Cav*, c. 200	10	10	34	54
Btty M, 1st NY Art, 6 guns & c. 60 (Best)	2	4	5	11
Btty F, Pa Art, 4 guns & c. 60 (Hampton)	0	7	4	11
Btty F, US 4 Art, 4 guns & c. 60	0	3	3	6
Unattached	6	17	135	154
10 Me, 856	3	6	54	63
Pa Zouaves D'Afrique, 120	1	1	2	4

8 *NY Cav*, c.300	2	5	24	31
Btty E, Pa Art	0	5	23	28

	KILLED	WOUNDED	MISSING	TOTAL
CONFEDERATE FORCES, c. 15,000	68	329	3	400
Maj. Gen. Thomas J. Jackson				
Jackson's Division				
Maj. Gen. Thomas J. Jackson				
1st Brigade, 1529 +	10	27	0	37
Brig. Gen. Charles Winder				
2 Va	4	14	0	18
4 Va	0	0	0	0
5 Va	1	3	0	4
27 Va	1	3	0	4
33 Va	1	7	0	8
2nd Brigade	2	14	0	16
Col. J.A. Campbell				
21 Va	0	0	0	0
42 Va	0	3	0	3
48 Va	2	7	0	9
1 Va Bn	0	4	0	4
3rd Brigade	2	34	0	36
Col. Samuel Fulkerson				
10 Va	1	8	0	9
23 Va	0	7	0	7
37 Va, c. 300	1	19	0	20
Artillery	3	21	0	24
Col. Stapleton Crutchfield				
Carpenter's Va Btty, 4 guns	1	5	0	6
Caskie's Va Btty, 4 guns	0	0	0	0
Cutshaw's Va Btty, 4 guns	0	0	0	0
Poague's Va Btty, 6 guns	2	16	0	18
Wooding's Va Btty, 4 guns	0	0	0	0
Ewell's Division	43	184	3	230
Maj. Gen. Richard S. Ewell				
2nd Brigade	0	0	0	0
Col. W.C. Scott				
44 Va	0	0	0	0

52 Va	0	0	0	0
58 Va	0	0	0	0
4th Brigade	0	0	0	0
Brig. Gen Arnold Elzey				
12 Ga	0	0	0	0
13 Va	0	0	0	0
25 Va	0	0	0	0
31 Va	0	0	0	0
7th Brigade	22	75	0	97
Brig. Gen. Isaac Trimble				
15 Ala.	0	0	0	0
21 Ga	1	16	0	17
16 Miss	0	0	0	0
21 NC	21	59	0	80
8th Brigade	21	109	3	133
Brig. Gen. Richard Taylor				
6 La	5	42	3	50
7 La	5	12	0	17
8 La	0	0	0	0
9 La	5	37	0	42
1 La Bn	1	6	0	7
Maryland Line	0	0	0	0
Brig. Gen. George Steuart				
1 Md	0	0	0	0
Baltimore Btty, 4 guns (Brockenbrough)	0	0	0	0
1 Coy Md Cav	0	0	0	0
Artillery				
Latimer's Va Btty, 6 guns				
Lusk's Va Btty, 4 guns				
Raines' Va Btty, 4 guns				
Rice's Va Btty, 4 guns				
Cavalry	11	15	0	26
Brig. Gen. Turner Ashby				
2 Va Cav				
6 Va Cav				
7 Va Cav				
Chew's Va Btty, 4 guns				

	Cross Keys *8 June 1862*			
	KILLED	WOUNDED	MISSING	TOTAL
UNION FORCES, c. 14,150	>114	>443	>127	>684
Maj. Gen. John C. Frémont				
Blenker's Division, c. 6450	>81	>295	>106	>482
Brig. Gen. Louis Blenker				
1st Brigade, 2750	68	239	90	397
Brig. Gen. Julius Stahel				
8 *NY*, 548	43	134	43	220
39 *NY*, c. 500	4	28	12	44
41 *NY*, c. 500	1	8	11	20
45 *NY*, c. 500	3	6	10	19
27 *Pa*, c. 500	17	61	14	92
2 *NY Btty*, c. 100 (Schirmer)	0	0	0	0
Btty C, WVa Art, c. 100 (Buell)	0	2	0	2
2nd Brigade, c. 1600—Col. John Koltes	0	1	8	9
29 *NY*, c. 500	0	1	6	7
68 *NY*, c. 500	0	0	2	2
73 *Pa*, c. 500	0	0	0	0
13 *NY Btty*, c.100	0	0	0	0
3rd Brigade, c. 1700—Brig. Gen. Henry Bohlen	13	52	8	73
54 *NY*, 373	1	4	0	5
58 *NY*, c. 400	7	18	4	29
74 *Pa*, c. 400	3	11	1	15
75 *Pa*, 375	2	16	3	21
Btty I, 1 NY Art, c. 100 (Wiedrich)	0	3	0	3
Divisional Cavalry, c. 400	0	0	0	0
4 *NY Cav*, c. 400	0	0	0	0
Advance Brigade, c.800	4	12	3	19
Col. Gustave Cluseret				
60 *Oh*, c. 400	3	4	0	7
8 *WVa*, c. 400	1	8	3	12
Milroy's Brigade, c. 2500	24	122	14	160
Brig. Gen. Robert Milroy				

2 *WVa*, c. 500	3	19	2	24
3 *WVa*, c. 500	4	23	0	27
5 *WVa*, c. 500	9	38	0	47
25 *Oh*, c. 500	6	40	5	51
1 *WVa Cav*, c. 200	0	0	7	7
Btty G, WVa Art, c. 100 (Ewing)	0	1	0	1
Btty I, 1 Oh Art, c. 100 (Hyman)	1	1	0	2
12 *Oh Btty*, c. 100 (Johnson)	1	0	0	1
Schenck's Brigade, 2436	4	7	4	15
Brig. Gen. Robert Schenck				
32 *Oh*, 500	0	1	0	1
55 *Oh*, 525	0	0	0	0
73 *Oh*, 295	4	3	0	7
75 *Oh*, 444	0	0	0	0
82 *Oh*, 374	0	2	0	2
1 *Conn Cav*, 113	0	0	4	4
Btty K, 1 Oh Art, 94 (DeBeck)	0	0	0	0
Rigby's Ind Btty, 91	0	1	0	1
Bayard's Cav Brigade, c. 1350	1	7	0	8
Brig. Gen. George Bayard				
1 *NJ Cav*, c. 500	0	0	0	0
1 *Pa Cav*, c. 600	0	0	0	0
13 *Pa Inf* (one bn), c. 150	1	7	0	8
2 *Me Btty*, c. 100 (Hall)	0	0	0	0
Unattached Cavalry, c. 600	0	0	0	0
6 *Oh Cav*, c. 400	0	0	0	0
3 *WVa Cav*, c. 200	0	0	0	0

	KILLED	WOUNDED	MISSING	TOTAL
CONFEDERATE FORCES, c. 7850	44	242	15	301
Maj. Gen. Thomas J. Jackson				
Jackson's Division (det), c.800	3	10	0	13
Maj. Gen. Thomas J. Jackson				
2nd Brigade, c. 800	3	10	0	13
Col. John Patton				
21 Va, c. 300 (unengaged)				
42 Va, c. 300	0	3	0	3

48 Va, c. 300	3	7	0	10
1 Va Bn, c. 200	0	0	0	0
Ewell's Division, c. 7050	41	232	15	288
Maj. Gen. Richard S. Ewell				
2nd Brigade, c. 1450	7	65	0	72
1 Md, c. 500	0	28	0	28
44 Va, 130	1	3	0	4
52 Va, c. 300	2	24	0	26
58 Va, c. 400	0	5	0	5
Brockenbrough's Md Btty, c. 50	2	0	0	2
Lusk's Va Btty c. 50	2	3	0	5
4th Brigade, c. 1450—Brig. Gen. Arnold Elzey (w)	6	33	9	48
12 Ga, c. 400	2	11	0	13
13 Va, c. 400	2	14	1	17
25 Va, c. 300	0	0	0	0
31 Va, 300	0	0	0	0
Raine's Va Btty, c. 50	2	7	8	17
7th Brigade, c. 1750—Brig. Gen. Isaac Trimble	23	109	6	138
15 Ala, c.400	9	37	5	51
21 Ga, c. 500	4	23	1	28
16 Miss, c. 400	6	28	0	34
21 NC, c. 400	2	11	0	13
Courtney's Va Btty, c. 50	2	10	0	12
8th Brigade, c. 2400—Brig. Gen. Richard Taylor	2	15	0	17
6 La, unengaged	0	0	0	0
7 La, c. 600	1	8	0	9
8 La, c. 500	1	7	0	8
9 La, unengaged	0	0	0	0
1 La Bn, unengaged	0	0	0	0

Port Republic			
9 June 1862			
	KILLED	WOUNDED	MISSING	TOTAL

	KILLED	WOUNDED	MISSING	TOTAL
UNION FORCES, c. 3450	68	360	510	940
Brig. Gen. James Shields				
3rd Brigade, c. 1627	51	214	431	696
Brig. Gen. Erastus Taylor				
5 *Oh*, c. 500	4	43	197	244
7 *Oh*, c. 327	10	55	10	75
29 *Oh*, c. 400	17	41	114	172
66 *Oh*, c. 400	20	75	110	205
4th Brigade, c. 1550	13	135	65	213
Col. Samuel S. Carroll				
7 *Ind*, c. 400	9	107	29	145
84 *Pa*, c. 300	1	10	21	32
110 *Pa*, c. 300	1	10	15	26
1 *WVa*, c. 400	0	0	0	0
1 *WVa Cav*, c. 400	2	8	0	10
Artillery, c. 300	4	13	14	31
Btty M, 1 Oh Art, c. 100 (Huntington)	2	4	5	11
Btty L, 1 Oh Art, c. 100 (Robinson)	1	4	6	11
Btty E, US 4 Art, c. 100 (Clark)	1	5	3	9

	KILLED	WOUNDED	MISSING	TOTAL
CONFEDERATE FORCES, 8670	91	697	36	824
Maj. Gen. Thomas J. Jackson				
Jackson's Division, c. 3750	13	164	32	209
Maj. Gen. Thomas J. Jackson				
1st Brigade, c. 1400—Brig. Gen. Charles Winder	13	145	31	189
2 Va, 224	1	24	0	25
4 Va, 317	0	4	0	4
5 Va, 447	4	89	20	113
27 Va, 150	8	28	11	47
33 Va, 260	0	0	0	0

2nd Brigade, c. 800—Col. J.A. Campbell	0	7	0	7
21 Va,		0		
42 Va, c. 300	0	0	0	0
48 Va, c. 300	0	7	0	7
1 Va Bn, c. 200	0	0	0	0
3rd Brigade, c. 1200—Brig. Gen. William B. Taliaferro	0	3	0	3
10 Va, c. 400	0	0	0	0
23 Va, c. 400	0	0	0	0
37 Va, c. 400	0	3	0	3
Artillery, c. 350	0	9	1	10
Carpenter's Va Btty, 70	0	4	0	4
Carrington's Va Btty	0	0	0	0
Caskie's Va Btty	0	1	0	1
Cutshaw's Va Btty	0	0	0	0
Poague's Va Btty, 71	0	4	1	5
Wooding's Va Btty	0	0	0	0
Ewell's Division, c. 4920	78	533	4	615
Maj. Gen. Richard S. Ewell				
2nd Brigade, c. 1220—Col. W.C. Scott	30	169	0	199
1 Md, c. 450	0	1	0	1
44 Va, c. 120	14	35	0	49
52 Va, c. 250	12	65	0	77
58 Va, c. 400	4	68	0	72
4th Brigade, c. 1400—Col. John Walker	15	109	4	128
12 Ga, c. 400	0	1	0	1
13 Va, c. 400	0	0	0	0
25 Va, 300	0	29	0	29
31 Va, 300	14	79	4	97
8th Brigade, c. 2400—Brig. Gen. Richard Taylor	33	255	0	288
6 La, c. 600	11	55	0	66
7 La, c. 600	8	115	0	123
8 La, c. 500	8	30	0	38
9 La, c. 500	4	36	0	40
1 La Bn, c. 200	2	19	0	21

Guide for the Interested Reader

Recommended Reading

Despite all the popularity and interest in Jackson's 1862 Shenandoah Valley Campaign, only two detailed studies of it have been written. The first was William Allan's *History of the Campaign of Gen. T J. (Stonewall) Jackson in the Shenandoah Valley of Virginia* (1880, reprinted 1974). Allan's work benefited greatly from his contacts with veterans of the campaign on both sides, particularly Jed Hotchkiss, Jackson's staff topographer, who provided Allan with the excellent maps for this study and loaned him his personal diary. Allan's work is excellent for its wealth of detailed information, particularly about army composition and strengths, but it understandably presents the Confederate side in more detail than the Union. A more balanced and detailed history of the campaign is Robert G. Tanner's *Stonewall in the Valley* (Garden City, 1976). This fine study is both analytical and descriptive, and is highly recommended to everyone, even though it does not answer with precision every question about the campaign.

Biographies

More typically, the campaign has been dealt with in the context of Jackson's life in the numerous biographies written about him. The greatest problem with the early biographers was their reverence for Jackson as a martyred hero and their idealization of his exploits and those of his men. Most notable of these was R. L. Dabney's *Life and Campaigns of Lieut. Gen. Thomas J.*

Jackson (New York, 1866). This work is strongly biased in favor of Jackson and the South, but it is filled with good primary source material since Dabney served as Stonewall's chief of staff in the Valley. John Esten Cooke's two biographies, *The Life of Stonewall Jackson* (New York, 1863), and *Stonewall Jackson, a Military Biography* (New York, 1866) are in the same vein. Cooke was also the author of *Stonewall Jackson and the Old Stonewall Brigade* (Charlottesville, 1954), which is too laudatory to be critical.

More recent biographers have been more objective, though all have been captivated by Jackson's personality and accomplishments. The most popular has perhaps been G. F. R. Henderson's *Stonewall Jackson and the American Civil War* (New York, 1898, with numerous later editions). Henderson's work is objective (he was an Englishman and had no ax to grind), though it is a product of the Victorian era. More recent thorough biographies of note are Burke Davis' *They Called Him Stonewall* (New York, 1954), Frank Vandiver's *Mighty Stonewall* (New York, 1957), and Lenoir Chambers' *Stonewall Jackson* (New York, 1959).

Another scholar who has dealt thoroughly with Jackson and his campaigns is Douglas S. Freeman in his classic works *R. E. Lee* (New York, 1934) and *Lee's Lieutenants* (New York, 1946). It was Freeman who delved into Jackson's physiological and psychological state during the Seven Days' Battles, an approach that Tanner took in his book for the last days of the Valley Campaign (*Stonewall in the Valley*, pages 358–360).

Without doubt the best source on Jackson's private life is the so-called *"Memoirs" of Stonewall Jackson*, which is actually a biography written by his wife Mary Anna Jackson (Louisville, 1895, reprinted 1976). This book was compiled thirty years after the war and is understandably not very critical. But it draws largely on Jackson's letters and personal papers, and as such provides a wealth of primary source material on Stonewall.

Additional first hand views of Jackson and his campaigns are provided by some of the men who lived and fought with him. The life of Jackson by Reverend Dabney, Stonewall's chief of staff, has already been mentioned. Two other staff officers wrote very informative memoirs. Henry Kyd Douglas, the youngest member of Stonewall's staff, wrote *I Rode with Stonewall* in 1866 and revised it in 1898-1899, but it was not published until 1940.

Douglas' work provides an extremely detailed account of Jackson's staff and campaigns. Equally informative is *Make Me a Map of the Valley*, the journal of Jed Hotchkiss, Stonewall's mapmaker (edited by Archie P. McDonald; Dallas, 1973.)

Jackson's Subordinates

Several of Jackson's soldiers wrote autographies about their roles in the Valley Campaign. By far the most notable of these is General Richard Taylor's *Destruction and Reconstruction* (New York, 1879). Taylor was an educated and articulate writer, and left a very clear account of his Louisiana brigade in the campaign. William T. Poague, captain of the Rockbridge Artillery, told of his services in *Gunner with Stonewall* (1957, reprinted 1987). Life in Jackson's infantry was very accurately described by John O. Casler in *Four Years in the Stonewall Brigade* (1893, with several recent reprints). Of equal stature is *One of Jackson's Foot Cavalry* by John H. Worsham of the 21st Virginia (New York, 1912, reprinted recently). A less detailed reminiscence is *The War* by James H. Wood of the 37th Virginia.

Additional primary source material can be found in the following standard reference works:

The War of the Rebellion, a Compilation of the Official Records of the Union and Confederate Armies (128 volumes; Washington, 1880–1901)

Southern Historical Society Papers (50 volumes; Richmond, 1876–1953)

Confederate Veteran (40 volumes; Nashville, 1893–1932)

Battles and Leaders of the Civil War (4 volumes; New York, 1884–1888, with several recent reprints) edited by Robert U. Johnson and Clarence C. Buel

Biographical sources on Jackson's subordinates are not numerous. The most notable of these is *The Life of Turner Ashby* by Thomas A. Ashby (New York, 1914, reprinted 1981). This work, though, is marred by hero worship. The same can be said of Percy Hamlin's *Old Bald Head*, a biography of Dick Ewell, Jackson's second-in-command in the Valley (Strasburg, VA, 1940). The role of many of Jackson's lieutenants can be seen in Freeman's *Lee's Lieutenants* (New York, 1946). Detailed careers of his colonels can be found in *Lee's Colonels* by Robert K. Krick

(Dayton, OH, 1984); the lives of Confederate Generals can be read in Ezra Warner's *Generals in Gray* (Baton Rouge, 1959).

Jackson's two most famous brigades have been the subject of significant studies. Highly recommended are James Robertson's *The Stonewall Brigade* (Baton Rouge, 1963) and *Lee's Tigers*, Terry L. Jones' study of the Louisiana regiments in Virginia (Baton Rouge, 1987). Studies of several individual regiments are also recommended:

> *The Maryland Line in The Confederate Army*, by W. W. Goldsborough (1900, reprinted 1983)
>
> *A History of the Laurel Brigade, Originally the Ashby Cavalry*, by William McDonald (1907, reprinted 1969)
>
> *History of Carpenter's Battery of the Stonewall Brigade*, by C. A. Fonerden (1911, reprinted 1983)

On the Opposition

Sources on the loyal opposition, the Union forces that opposed Jackson, are not nearly as numerous as those from the Confederate side. No studies of the campaign have been written from the Union viewpoint; it was even passed over in Scribner's Campaigns of the Civil War series published in the 1880s. For an excellent account of the 1864 Shenandoah Valley Campaign, see *Sheridan in the Shenandoah* by E. J. Stackpole (Harrisburg, 1961).

The following biographies of Jackson's leading opponents are recommended:

> *Fighting Politician, Major General Nathaniel N. P. Banks*, by F. H. Harrington (1948, reprinted 1970)
>
> *Fremont, Explorer for a Restless Nation*, by Ferol Egan (Garden City, 1977)
>
> *Life of Major General James Shields*, by William H. Loudon (Chicago, 1900)

Battle Accounts

From the viewpoint of the fighting man, the best battle accounts can be found in the numerous regimental histories published after the war. Representative of these are the following studies of units involved in the 1862 Valley Campaign:

> *Ride to War, the History of the First New Jersey Cavalry*, by Henry R. Pyne (1871, reprinted 1961)
>
> *Historical Record of the First Maryland Infantry*, by Charles Camper (Washington DC, 1971)

History of the 9th Regiment of New York Cavalry, by Newel Cheney
(Jamestown, NY, 1901)

History of the 4th Regiment of Ohio Volunteers, by William Kepler
(Cleveland, 1886)

History of the 7th Ohio, by George L. Wood (1869, reprinted 1958)

*Carl Bornemann's Regiment, the 41st New York Infantry in the Civil
War,* by David G. Martin (1987)

Sidelights

For additional sidelights on the campaign, the following
books are recommended:

One Hundred Years at V.M.I., by William Couper (Richmond, 1939)

A History of the Valley of Virginia, by Samuel Kercheval (Strasburg,
VA, 1925)

The Baltimore and Ohio in the Civil War, by Festus P. Summers
(New York, 1939)

Simulations and War Games

The following are the best of the wargames produced on the
subject of the Valley Campaign:

"Stonewall, the Battle of Kernstown," published by Simulations
Publications in 1978

"Jackson at the Crossroads, Cross Keys & Port Republic," published by Simulations Publications in 1981

"Shenandoah, a Civil War Game of the Valley Campaigns, 1862
and 1864," published by Battleline Publications in 1975

Poetry

Of the many poems written on Jackson and his men, by far the
most popular was "Stonewall Jackson's Way" (see text). After
his untimely death, M. Deeves composed the somber "Stonewall
Jackson's Requiem" (see text).

Historical Parks

Unfortunately, all of Jackson's battles in the Shenandoah
Valley in 1862 were on too small a scale to merit present-day
preservation in state or national parks. Thus his great deeds at
Kernstown, McDowell, Winchester, Cross Keys and Port Republic are marked today only by a few state and local historical
markers.

Index